What readers are saying about *Dance into the Light*:

"A profoundly touching memoir that is a must-read for anyone who has cared deeply about a loved one. Brewer openly shares her vulnerabilities as she repeatedly attempts to rescue her sister. She candidly shares life lessons learned as she moves beyond the darkness."

—**Susan Blue**, R.N. (Retired Nurse Manager) and Co-host of Podcast Series - *Stories from the Field*

"A compelling and poignant memoir; Brewer's heart-centred exploration of the human condition is raw and real, forcing the reader to confront their own inner demons (and come out the other side better for having done so). This is a must-read, not only for anyone who has suffered a loss, but also for everyone who has faced adversity with a loved one."

—**Cindy Watson**, award-winning and best-selling author of *The Art of Feminine Negotiation* and *Out of Darkness*.

"An intimate study of one sister's lifelong efforts to re-establish family unity and forge new bonds. Nearly swallowed by anguish in a time of family tragedy, the loving supports of her aging father and ailing husband carry her through. The author shares her despair by journaling thoughts from a place of deep faith. Readers will cheer as she finds her way, learning that to be vulnerable is to be human."

—**Sheridan Rondeau**, author of *Dear Braveheart: a Caregiver's Loving Journey Through Alzheimer's Dementia.*

"This raw and honest memoir reveals the tenacity of the human spirit with the most dreaded outcome. Illustrating deep love and unwavering determination to save a sister, Bev rediscovers life after traumatic loss. Full of quiet wisdom, *Dance into the Light* is a beautifully written and incredibly poignant story."

—**Yvonne Heath**, author, speaker, founder of *Love Your Life to Death.*

DANCE INTO THE LIGHT

a memoir

by

Beverley Brewer

blue denim press

Dance into the Light

Copyright © 2023 Beverley Brewer

All rights reserved

Published by Blue Denim Press Inc.

First Edition

ISBN - 978-1-927882-83-2

No part of this book may be used or reproduced in any manner whatsoever without written permission except in the case of brief quotations embodied in critical articles or reviews.

This is a work of non-fiction. Except for the author's immediate family, fictional names have been used for privacy reasons.

Cover Image—thumb/istock.com

Cover Design—Shane Joseph

Library and Archives Canada Cataloguing in Publication
    Title: Dance into the Light : a memoir / by Beverley Brewer.
    Names: Brewer, Beverley, author.
    Description: First edition. | Includes bibliographical references.
    Identifiers: Canadiana (print) 20230491480 | Canadiana (ebook) 20230491499 | ISBN 9781927882832 (softcover) | ISBN 9781927882849 (Kindle) | ISBN 9781927882856 (EPUB) | ISBN 9781927882863 (IngramSpark EPUB)
    Subjects: LCSH: Brewer, Beverley. | LCSH: Brewer, Beverley—Family. | LCSH: Brewer, Beverley—Childhood and youth. | LCSH: Sisters—Family relationships. | LCSH: Suicide victims—Family relationships. | LCSH: Sisters—Death. | LCSH: Sisters—Biography. | LCSH: Bereavement. | LCSH: Families. | LCGFT: Autobiographies.
    Classification: LCC HV6545.9 .B74 2023 | DDC 362.28/3—dc23

Dedication

Dad and Jack, my two rocks.

Table of Contents

Prologue
A Letter 1

One
The Beginning as the Ending 3

Two
Baby Jacquelin 13

Three
Lost Days 15

Four
Seven Days in the ICU 27

Five
Another Diagnosis 39

Six
An Unresolved Dance with Suicide Loss 42

Seven
Help Came My Way 52

Eight
Phone Call to a New Friend 59

Nine
A Falling Out Between the Cracks 82

Ten
A Blessing 89

Eleven
 A Meeting of Weeping Strangers 100

Twelve
 Telling Dad Six Days Later 102

Thirteen
 Watching From the Street... 108

Fourteen
 Soft Places to Land 111

Fifteen
 Jacquelin's Funeral 114

Sixteen
 A Deathtrap... 119

Seventeen
 More Wise Women 134

Eighteen
 Me As Outlier.. 137

Nineteen
 Support, Confrontation, and, the Fat Lil' Book 146

Twenty
 A Writing Assignment Becomes a Treasure 152

Twenty-one
 Friendship in the Midst of Trees 163

Twenty-two
 Wine for Breakfast.. 168

Twenty-three
Pass over the Phone 171

Twenty-four
A Painful Cottage Visit 182

Twenty-five
Looking for Answers in the Literature 184

Twenty-six
Tough Love is Harder Than It Sounds 190

Twenty-seven
Labour Day Weekend 200

Twenty-eight
The Ending as the Beginning 202

Epilogue
Lessons in the Light 214

Acknowledgements   222

Bibliography   223

Author Bio   224

Dance into the Light

Prologue
A Letter

November 16, 2017

Dear Jacquelin,
 Had you told me you were thinking of ending your life, I would have stood in your way. You didn't like it when I stood in your way. On one occasion I thought you were going to hit me. You weren't yourself that day. While you were screaming at me, I ran to Dad's chair and fell to prayer, and you said, "That's not going to help you." But it did. I went outside to trim the trees and catch my breath and let you catch yours. Then I came back, put on the kettle and made tea. We didn't say much, just drank our tea.

On September 6, 2017, my deepest fear for you came to realization. You left, and you did it for good. Final. No more second chances for either of us. No more time to reconstruct words so that you might hear differently.

You must have thought about it, that is, I can only guess you took the time to think about your choice to give up on everything. You gave up on all of us.

Forever love, Bev.

[My notes from a workshop at the Distress Centre Conference in Toronto.]

***

Four months earlier on a grey afternoon on my father's backyard deck Jacquelin's voice had escalated so loud I felt self-conscious. My concern was grounded in my late-mother's anxiety about giving the neighbours something to talk about. I suggested we take our discussion inside and, Jacquelin—still shouting—followed me into the house. I had never seen her like that before. Rage contorted her face. She was scaring me. I hurried into the living room toward my father's chair. Jacquelin's hands leaned on the chair's armrests and she loomed over me inches away from my face. To protect myself from her words and the actions I feared she might take I buried my head into my arms and prayed for help. That was not the first or last time I prayed for help for my youngest sister.

While I fought to rescue my youngest sister from what I perceived to be her life's darkness, I was also grieving the loss of my mother, walking alongside my husband in his unfolding cancer journey, and witnessing my father's strength and independence dwindle.

Given my propensity to fix other people's lives and the fact that Jacquelin's life in her forties and into her early fifties had almost become my own, I had to keep reminding myself that I was not writing a biography about my sister. I couldn't; I didn't know her as well as I thought, and this memoir is about becoming myself, not second-guessing my sister.

I have thought deeply about my sister's challenges and the reasons for her final choice. I have also pondered our relationship and how impossible I found it to extricate myself from her life. Before she died, when I inserted my presence back into her unyielding and chaotic life—mostly uninvited—I found myself standing on uncertain ground. I wanted to rescue her but I didn't expect to abandon myself. The seven-year struggle was immense. In my personal journals I grasped at hints of light in the despair surrounding my youngest sister's suicide.

To the reader accompanying me on this journey, I wish to say that the timeline of grief is not the linear timeline of our lives. Memories come from all directions and from different times, *at* different times. The picture I paint of Jacquelin, and, our relationship, will therefore be as fragmented as her life was.

One
The Beginning as the Ending

September 5 - 6, 2017

When we arrived at my dad's house, Jacquelin's treasured black Audi was in the driveway. Jack turned off the ignition and I tried not to clench my jaw. The two front windows were cranked wide open and every light in the front of the house was on.

"Wow, the house is lit up like a candle," I said.

"Yeah, your dad would have a fit," said Jack.

"That's for sure," I said, reciting his much-repeated motto, "Waste not, want not."

Jack pulled in behind Jacquelin's car, and I jumped out of the jeep.

"I won't be long. I just want to have a quick word."

I walked up the stairs anticipating I'd find Jacquelin smoking on the brown-leather love seat in the den in front of the television. The coffee table within her reach would be cluttered with nail polish, files, and skin moisturizers. A cigarette would sit in an over-filled ashtray beside a glass of water.

I considered my greeting. "Hey Jacq, how you doing?"

Like other times she'd look my way and tell me she was "okay."

I knocked on the door at the same time I inserted my key. I didn't hear the little click. When I turned the key, I didn't feel the usual tension in my wrist. The door wasn't locked.

Inside the vestibule, I called her name.

"Jacquelin."

Jacquelin's Portuguese Waterdog pup, Siron came around the corner. He dragged his belly close to the floor and his ears were wet and appeared pinned to his head.

I touched his furry head. "Ah Siron, what's wrong? Where's your mother?"

The room was unusually bright. Jacquelin must have changed the bulbs from my dad's preference—forty watts— to one-hundred. For as long as I could remember I'd heard their disagreements about lightbulbs. She accused him of being "cheap."

The kitchen glistened. *She's been cleaning. Maybe she's feeling better.*

The counter was no longer cluttered. There was only a bread knife, a French loaf, and a half-eaten tomato and cheese sandwich on a plate.

"Jacquelin?"

No answer.

I walked down the bungalow's hallway. She wasn't in the bathroom.

Light shone from under her bedroom door. Not wanting to scare her, I brushed my knuckles across the door. Inside I saw the stripped bed. The duvet had no cover and drawers of all three dressers were open.

I'd made a suggestion a week earlier. "Tidy up your room Jacq, it will help to make you feel better."

With the possibility of a new job, she needed an airy place to hang up her clothes so they didn't get creased. Our dad had moved into his nursing home nine days earlier.

"Put your clothes into Dad's closet. Your suits can breathe. I'll help you if you want."

The door to my dad's bedroom was open, as usual. Her clothes, still on their hangers, were piled on the bed. She'd started the task of shifting her clothes. Good for her.

I stood at the threshold of the den, the little room that was once my bedroom. A space where I felt cozy and safe. After my mom died in December of 2013, the den underwent another transition and became the place where Dad passed the time watching television. Since my dad stopped using his workshop in the basement, he kept a tool box in the corner. The only light in the room was from the glow of the television screen.

To the left of the doorway, I saw what looked like a wig of long brown hair on a pole. I had difficulty making sense out of the image—a wig on a pole?

What am I seeing?

I'm not sure how many seconds it took before reality hit.

It's not a wig...Actual hair...Jacquelin's.

My sister's head was slumped forward, her body draped across the cushioned dog bed in front of the closet door. Her hair covered her face. Her bare feet were lifeless. Everything appeared out of whack and nothing looked real.

It looked like a movie set. Eventually...what I was seeing became real. Horrifyingly real.

I screamed her name. "Jacquelin." Once my legs caught up to my brain, I lunged toward her. I held her face. Her skin was cold.

In a softer voice I asked, "Jacquelin, what have you done? Jacquelin, what have you done?"

Then I saw the cord. It was red, looped over the top of the door, and reached around to a small screw that stuck out an inch.

My knees buckled and I fell to the floor.

Rising with great effort, I ran to the front door and yelled into the driveway at Jack. I can't be sure how many times I screamed into the driveway.

"A lot," Jack told me later.

Jack rushed into the house. I tried to be clear so he could understand what I was saying. "She's not breathing."

As Jack rushed down the hall toward the den, he said, "Call 911."

When I spoke to a woman dispatcher, I did my best to be understood. "I just found my sister. She's hanging from the door."

She asked me my name. She had a low voice and it was calm. She helped me think straight.

"You need to cut her down," said the woman. "Give her artificial respiration. Do you know how to do that?"

"Yes." It had been a long time, but I knew I could to do it.

Calmly, Jack stood beside me in the kitchen. I hadn't heard him step up beside me where I was using the landline.

Gently, he told me. "She's dead. She's cold. She's been gone a while. . . . AR isn't going to help."

"But the woman on the phone said—"

He was patient with me. He took the phone from my hand and spoke to the dispatcher. After he hung up the phone, I followed him to the den. Like the dispatcher had instructed, he laid Jacquelin on her back.

I saw my sister's face. No life. No colour. Her eyes were closed and her mouth looked funny.

I was frantic. Jack held me. I remember pushing him away because I had to find Siron.

Firefighters came to the house. The paramedics came soon after. They asked questions with serious faces.

"When did you last see her? When did you last speak to her?"

I had a hard time remembering. I was unhinged and frantic. I thought about God.

The police came. Sergeants. Plain clothes. Same questions.

I started tidying the kitchen. I wanted to empty the trash, and then I was politely told to leave everything. My father's house had become a crime scene.

"Crime scene?"

The policeman nodded. "Everything looks straightforward, but we still have to rule out homicide."

Hearing the word homicide gave me a jolt. After she started to drink, Jacquelin's life had filled with strangers, and she let them into her house. *They stole from her. Broke her things. And God knows what else.* I thought of the bad people in her life and pushed the thought of homicide away.

I went to the couch near the window. Other than the dim street lamp by the driveway, the outside was dark and quiet. There were no lights on at the neighbours' but that didn't mean no one was watching. Had my mother been there, that would have been top of mind because she always worried about being judged or evaluated by other people.

The police officer returned from the den. He would have seen where Jack had carefully laid Jacquelin on the floor.

He held her phone in his hand.

"I see your texts."

"Yes. I've been trying to connect with her all night."

He nodded.

"I found these keys. They were on the floor."

"They're mine," I said. "They must have dropped from my hand."

"I also found a note," he said.

"She left a note?" I was surprised she had taken the time to write a note. "Can I see it?"

"Not yet," he said softly. "It's evidence."

Disappointed, I told him I understood.

The officer said, "I'll need to take your keys to the house."

He said we couldn't return to the house until after there was a full investigation. Each time the police officer used the words "investigation" and "evidence" a wave of nausea moved through my stomach.

As the night went on, people came and went. The fire department arrived first. Then the EMS. *Or maybe it was the police, I'm not remembering clearly.* I watched every person as if they were a character in a screenplay. Each person offered us their deepest sympathies. I still haven't forgotten their respectful care and how in those sad and confusing moments, I didn't feel alone.

***

Two more officers came—plain clothes detectives—a male and female. They repeated what the firefighters and paramedics had said, "Sorry for your loss," and then like everyone else, they disappeared down the hallway.

The female detective returned to the living room where I was sitting with Siron on the couch.

"I think I've been here before," she said.

I recognized her, "Yes. You were in uniform then."

She said she'd been recently promoted.

"Congratulations," I said. "You were here twice. Once after I reported my sister as missing. And before that, when she broke into my dad's house. I might not have that quite right."

"That's okay." Her voice was kind and supportive.

"Since you were last here, she'd gotten dry and reconciled with my father," I said.

What she said next made my heart ache.

"We found an empty vodka bottle…a mickey…in the room."

"You found alcohol?"

"Yes." She brought the bottle she'd been holding from behind her back.

My heart sank even deeper. Then things started to come together. She started to drink again. It explained why she hadn't made it to my dad's nursing home on the weekend. No driving with booze in her system, I thought. Her breathalyzer wouldn't allow it. The empty bottle explained her silence.

I called my sister, Melody. When she answered, I heard loud happy music in the background.

"What?" Loud music…"What'd you say?" Loud music…

My nerves were raw. I just wanted her to listen...turn the music down...Then I told her.

She sobbed and wheezed for air. "Jacquelin's dead?"

The music stopped.

"Yes."

"She killed herself?"

"Yes. She took her life." The words in my answer didn't feel right.

While we were still talking, the detective called me away from the phone. She needed me to verify Jacquelin's birthdate.

"February 10, 1966."

She wanted proof.

I hung up the phone from Mel to find Jacquelin's license inside her purse. She had a full pack of cigarettes and forty dollars in cash. Inside, I also found the two of my mother's change purses, full of loonies and toonies. It didn't look like Jacquelin used any of the money. I was noticing small details like that.

Not knowing where Jack was at the time or what to do with myself, I shuffled around the kitchen. There was fresh food in the fridge, which meant Jacquelin had gone shopping. I fed Siron and added water to his bowl. I tried to encourage him to go out, but he had already left a small mess on the carpet. He didn't want to leave my side.

Mel called back, crying hard. Hysterical. She asked if Jacquelin had really killed herself.

"Yes. She's gone, Mel...Do you want to come here?"

"Yes."

"Come then." I told her she could stay at our place if she wanted.

One of the officers had called the coroner. "There's only one working in the city tonight. It could be a long night," he said.

Mel and her husband Owen arrived by cab.

The male detective urged her not to go into the den. He looked over at me and added, "It's pretty tough. A tragic scene. You won't want to remember your sister like that."

Mel made it clear that she had no intention of going into the den.

Thanks to my mother's proclivity for hospitality and insisting on having more than enough seating, the living room held a love seat, a long couch and an assortment of easy chairs and if that wasn't enough, the piano bench. The rocker, by the window opposite the couch where my mom always sat, was my dad's favourite place to sit. When my niece Marianne and her husband Tim arrived, there was a seat for everyone.

At around four o'clock in the morning the coroner arrived. I was sitting on the end of the couch in the living room closest to the window again. He knelt down beside me and looked into my eyes.

"I'll examine her here but do a more thorough examination at the coroner's office."

"Okay."

Jack watched me. Later, he told me he was worried about me.

I felt the weight of Jack's hand on my back. He whispered in my ear. He said he needed to go home and let our dogs out. We'd left home over twelve hours ago and they would need a backyard break. I'd forgotten all about them.

"Yes, go," I said.

He brushed my face with his fingers. "I'll come right back and get you."

I recall being unsure about ever wanting to leave my dad's house again. Under the circumstances, leaving was too final.

Disoriented, I observed Jack back his jeep out onto the street. He didn't make his regular turn. I wondered if he was worrying about his next oncology appointment. He usually went right and when he drove the other way, I realized I'd forgotten to remind him to drive with care like I always did and I worried something else awful could happen in the absence of my words.

I whispered toward the window. "Jack, please drive careful. There's no need to rush." If anyone heard me mutter, they didn't say.

The windows were still open and the earlier smell in the house was gone. Most of the lights Jacquelin had left on had been turned off. Everything around me was big and exaggerated. The tick from my mother's old favourite clock seemed louder than usual. Mel's face was swollen from tears. I tried to balance my mind between clarity and sorrow. It felt like there was too much space between me and everyone else. Nothing was right.

The coroner returned to the living room. "A team from the city's morgue is on their way," he said. "When I get back to the morgue, I'll complete my examination and write up my report."

I closed my eyes and nodded.

"Again, very sorry for your loss."

With fewer people, the atmosphere in the house changed again and became more somber. Even the pup was subdued. Sad too, I thought.

Mel broke the silence with a cough. "This is going to be really hard on Dad," she said. "How do you think we should tell him?"

"We need to tell him together."

When I wandered back into the kitchen I thought about the tomato sandwich, half-eaten. What stopped Jacquelin from eating the whole thing? Beside the plate on the green counter was a paring knife, and beside that, stuck to the counter, dried tomato seeds. The kitchen scene was unchanged since I found Jacquelin and I had an urge to wipe the counter but remembered the officer's words.

"Don't touch anything. This is a crime scene."

Mesmerized by the dried tomato seeds, I tried to fathom what was happening.

He had said, "Leave everything as it is…"

No. I wanted to do something useful, something tangible. What I really wanted to do was to turn back the clock that hung over the door in my parent's beloved kitchen.

I closed my eyes. I needed to create space to make sense of things.

Two

Baby Jacquelin

February 10, 1966

When I was eleven years old, during Show and Tell, I told my classmates that I have a new baby sister. "Her name is Jacquelin Mary."

I didn't tell them it was love at first sight. From the time my mother brought Jacquelin home from the hospital, I was swallowed in emotion I didn't understand. Many times since, the same visceral pulses have bubbled to the surface. A Greek word providing a more apt explanation is "splagchnizomai," which literally means "to be moved so deeply by something that you feel it in the pit of your stomach." The word also entails the urge to act on behalf of the person you feel deeply about.

Jacquelin didn't mind that I liked to fuss over her hair, her clothes, and what she ate. When she was little, she let me take care of her. With lots of experience at diaper-changing, bathing, feeding, and scouting out Melody's missing soothers, mothering Jacquelin came easily. I was already accustomed to the protocols of carriage walks—proper harnessing, keeping baby's head covered at all times and, when stationary, engage the brake. Unfortunately, there was one incident never to be repeated. My thirteen-year-old self should have known better than to pull the carriage, with Jacquelin in it, up the porch stairs. Something went terribly wrong and two-year-old Jacquelin bounced, face first, onto the sidewalk. Within seconds, her forehead swelled into the shape of an oversized egg, and beyond worrying she might be dead, I feared her beautiful face—blue eyes with blonde curls framing fair skin—would be forever disfigured. In a short time, her face was fine.

My mother was relaxed about the whole incident. She said Jacquelin was an easy baby, and on the day I dropped my sister on her head, I had to agree. My mother demonstrated her adoration of her youngest and most beautiful child—apparently the perfect birth—by assigning playful nicknames to daughter number three. In my mother's most lovable moments, Jacquelin was Bubaca or Dukabor, mostly shortened to Duke or Dukie. Neither Mel nor I were ever given a nickname, which, by the way, I accepted—then and now— as a saving grace. I suspected Mel, middle child and six years older than Jacquelin, might have liked a special name too, besides "Melo-monster."

Early mothering by me extended into Jacquelin's toddler years. She was lovable, and when I took her places her clever quips entertained my friends. Her wit received high praise. Her sarcasm too—until someone got embarrassed.

"Kids her age aren't supposed to be so mouthy," said my friend Bill.

Or saucy. Or smart.

Her smart curiosity drew me in. One time, I found her in my room leafing through the glossy pictures in a first-year university book called, *Death in the Middle Ages*. I was struck by her keen inquisitiveness in pictures that captured those dark times with a great deal of violence. She gravitated to comic books that would never have interested me—horror, guts, and gore. At the time, while I embraced her interest in reading, I thought her choices a tad strange. When I told a friend, she said her brother liked those comics too and she assured me Jacquelin's choices were "normal."

Three

Lost Days

September 7, 8 and 9, 2017

Thursday

Eight restless hours after I found Jacquelin, I texted my minister, Reverend Ian LaFleur. In the morning's silence, I wrote that there had been a tragedy and asked him to call me when he could. He phoned me right away. Later that same day, he came to our house and sat with us. I told him I hadn't spoken to my father yet. I said Mel and I wanted to talk to him together. With Jack.

"I was wondering if you could be there too," I said.

"Of course."

I asked him to officiate her funeral service.

"Of course."

Ian suggested I take some time to think about what readings, prayers, and hymns I would like for the service.

I told him I had two favourites and I hummed the tune of the hymn *Sister, Let Me Be Your Servant* (also known as the *Servant Song*). The hymn always caused me to think about my relationship with Jacquelin. When we were much younger, I could tell what was going on with Jacquelin. Like my mother had with me, I had a sixth sense of when Jacquelin was troubled. I would phone her when I had a hunch. Sometimes I'd get a clue during one of my long telephone conversations with my mom. When Jacquelin drank heavily and slipped into darkness, I couldn't read her anymore. The thought of losing her scared me and that's why the *Servant Song's* lyrics pulled at my heart.

The theme of reciprocity in this hymn was what I longed for in my relationship with my sister Jacquelin.

Ian's warm brown eyes never left my face. He nodded. "That hymn will work."

"I also love *She Comes Sailing on the Wind*."

Another thoughtful nod. "Yes. That works too."

The tender lyrics, a phrase about a mother exhaling life into a child, never failed to stab at my heart. In those darker days I could hardly stop thinking about her. Jacquelin's life settled into my head.

Closer to the beginning of my sister's problems a woman I knew from my church and Pilates classes, invited me to join a program she ran called *Seasons of the Soul*. I had no idea what I was getting into but my intuition told me I needed to show up. Elizabeth's intensity intrigued me and our relationship held qualities of friendship—trust, loyalty, empathy. She was an accomplished artist. At each of our sessions, she limbered the five of us up with music, poetry, and scripture readings, followed by prayer and meditation. *Seasons of the Soul* reacquainted me with my fondness to work with my hands. She had us working various art media—beads, bread dough, paint, pastels and charcoal—and she encouraged us to journal, which for me was already part of my daily life.

In pastels I drew two images on a large piece of paper. Soft classical music played in the background while we worked. Afterwards, I picked up my journal and wrote:

Two images in one. A Freudian slip of the brush? A woman with tears. Who? Me or Jacquelin?

At the time of my enrolment in *Seasons*, Jacquelin's life was particularly worrisome. I carried her troubles with me, and when I later studied my own masterpiece—just kidding—I wrote:

Me, crying tears for her. No…the image is her crying her own pain. Tears that hold regret and fear and aloneness. Abandonment…I see myself in the image. I see her too. Tears. Fear. Abandonment. One image that could be two.

My intuition went into overdrive, especially in contemplative settings like church or while at the cottage paddling a kayak through a marsh. Even though the intuitive hunches were painfully honest, I nurtured them. My meandering thoughts about Jacquelin were not all bad, sad, or bleak. When she was working hard to stay sober and get back into the workforce, she continued to be front and centre in my prayers.

Raw and numb after finding Jacquelin the way I did, I reached out to lifelong friends—Joyce and Susan and my cousin Cathy. I caught Susan a few minutes before she had to leave for work. Joyce lived down the street from my dad's house and was flabbergasted about the unheard commotion— fire truck, ambulance, numerous police cars, and finally, the shiny black hearse—that happened while she slept.

"Why didn't you call me?" asked Joyce.

"It was late…"

"Does your dad know?"

"Not yet," I said.

"Are you going to be okay?"

"I think so…probably…yeah…I think I'll be okay."

"Hmmmm. What can I do to help?"

"I have an appointment at the funeral home for Friday and Jack has to be at the hospital for chemo. Will you come with me?"

"Of course."

Later in the day, I spoke to my aunt and asked her to tell my cousins. Afterwards, I went next door and wept in my neighbours' living room. Even though friends had other places to be, the conversations took as long as they needed. Their hearts were broken too. They wanted a different conclusion to Jacquelin's story of struggle. Each friend offered to call another friend and everyone told me to take care of myself.

But I was afraid to put my head down. If I closed my eyes, the stark image of Jacquelin as I found her flashed into my mind. Sleep did not come easily. When it came, it was scary. My body thrusted me from prone to sitting upright in bed. It was hard to understand the strength of the force or where it came from. Sometimes involuntary movements threw me onto the floor. Jack woke every time. He brought me back to bed and rubbed my back until I stopped shaking. He held me and let me cry. Sobs swelled from my diaphragm and up through my gut. My throat felt raw. During the daytime, napping was an impossibility. I was too pumped. When I did sleep, it had to be with the light on.

***

I could not forget that my dad still did not know about her death. Convinced we needed to tell him in the best way possible, I started with a phone call to the nursing home's director. There were still aspects of the nursing home I felt unsure about, and the soon-to-be-out-going director was one of them. I had recently encountered a time when she publicly lashed out at one of her staff. It was an embarrassing moment in the main floor lobby when everyone looked away. I questioned her professional judgement and ability to empathize, never mind be compassionate. I regretted she was the person I had to speak to about my father's devasting loss.

"I'm hoping there is a private space where we can tell my dad—"

She said all the right things and she promised to call me with an answer.

"Wednesday, September 12 at one o'clock."

A six-day wait and only one day before the funeral. Nothing about waiting that length of time felt right. I pictured the alternative: Mel,

Jack, Reverend Ian and me crowded in my father's room with only a curtain separating us from his room-mate.

The stern director must have picked up on my disappointment. "It's the best I can do."

It wasn't her fault the nursing room had outgrown its capacity. So far there had been many letdowns about my father's care and this felt like one more. I was still reeling over his recent twenty-one day stay in the hospital where the physiotherapists appeared to have given up on him and the doctor kept repeating my father's age.

"Yes, I know, how old my father is," I said.

Weighing on me was my dad's disappointment about not returning to his own home. It would not have been safe, so I had to find him a nursing home where his growing medical needs could be met. Fewer than three weeks before Jacquelin's death, I rode with him in the back of an ambulance to a nursing home that wasn't anyone's choice.

I ended the call with the director and turned to the task of leaving detailed messages for Mel and Reverend Ian. Feeling pushed to carry on, I felt satisfied inserting fresh checkmarks into my notebook's expanding list of "People to Call." Mel was also making phone calls. Jack too.

***

The funeral was three days away and I wanted my sister's service to be intimate and personal. I asked for help from people who would not carry unforgiving judgement about her final decision. My friend Jan knew the hymns and agreed to play the piano. Joanne, a gifted singer who had reached out to Jacquelin, said she would sing two solos.

Mel's not a church person, so she was okay with me pulling together the threads in planning Jacquelin's funeral. Being in the liturgy grounded me. All the talking I did on the phone with the people whom I knew loved Jacquelin, breathed life into my weary soul.

Friday

I opened my laptop and wrote an email...

Friday, September 8, 2017, 7:07 a.m.

Subject: I want you to know

Dear Friends,

Each of you is a treasured friend from my past Seneca life. Our paths have crossed in so many meaningful ways. We have shared and listened. I feel blessed to be holding your wisdom in my heart. You have heard me talk about my sister Jacquelin and some of the many ways I have tried to steer her into a more contented life. My deep love for my sister, who often times felt like my daughter, carried me through these challenges. Jacquelin ended her life a couple of days ago. I don't really know how to write about all of this yet. It's so complex...my dad doesn't know yet. I worry about telling him she's gone while he's in a nursing home surrounded by strangers. I'm giving myself time to let the tragic images soften. Victim Services tells me it will take a long time...

I am going to the funeral home today. I don't know what my sister's wishes are. She may have a will, likely not...calling a lawyer...and if she doesn't, how do I decide about arrangements for her death, especially without my dad's input? So far, I'm following some aspects of the imprint of my mother's funeral in 2013. I am trusting myself.

Jack is going in for a treatment today (every two weeks now)...immunotherapy is working for him. His last MRI report was very good. I am thankful beyond words.

I would love to hear your voice, see your face sometime in the future, or read your wise words on the page.

Your loving friend,

Bev

Jack had his usual ten o'clock morning appointment for bloodwork followed by chemo. I needed to be at the funeral home and had no idea how long it would take. Being in two places at once was an impossibility and neither Jack nor I had an easy time asking people for help.

"Our friends have been telling us they want to help...Should we ask Bob or Jon to drive you to the hospital?"

Bob was quick to respond to our request.

About one hour into the appointment at the funeral home, Joyce and I shared a glance acknowledging the oddity of the clerk's way of talking—flat and slow in a robotic fashion. For my benefit, Joyce succinctly paraphrased his convoluted instructions.

When the female worker muttered something about the aftermath of autopsies, Joyce said, "I don't think my friend needs to hear that right now."

On the way back to Joyce's house she told me something I had totally missed. The woman had made a disparaging remark about the nature of Jacquelin's death, and Joyce had felt compelled to shut her down. Her description of discretely kicking the woman's leg underneath the table made me laugh.

At home, I checked in with Jack and felt compelled to repeat how lots of fluids washed chemo out of his system. I told him the date for the funeral, Wednesday, September 13, and when I wrote that detail into my own calendar, I was reminded of a get-together with my writing partner, Gail. We agreed, instead to meet over coffee. We would see one another in the chapel. Shocked and saddened by my news, Gail told me to call her when I was feeling ready to pack up Jacquelin's stuff.

Off the phone from Gail, I told Jack all about the funeral home people.

"Remember Lurch in *The Adams Family?*" He did. "Yeah well, the guy at the funeral home looked kind of like him."

"Hmmm. Wonderful."

I told him why Joyce kicked the woman under the table.

"I hope it was a good swift boot."

It was good to laugh some more.

Later on in the evening, Jack encouraged me to pour a glass of wine. "It might help you relax."

Never before had I been afraid of the dark, and when he encouraged me to go to bed early, I did not mention that sleep was no longer appealing.

***

Saturday

After catching my reflection in the mirror, I called the salon. I thought a haircut might do a little to raise my spirits, which is what I had hoped for Jacquelin. Only seven days earlier— in preparation for her fourth level interview— I had treated Jacquelin to a cut-and-colour at the same salon. When I arrived, I heard how the owner, her daughter, and the stylist had enjoyed meeting my sister.

"Your sister is lovely," said the owner. "Does she like her cut?"

I felt obliged to tell them she had died.

"She took her own life."

They extended deeper sympathies and later at the wash station the stylist whispered me her blunt question.

"How did she do it?"

I understood her curiosity, but the question was too soon and too brazen. I wasn't shy talking about the details of Jacquelin's death, but revealing any more to a stranger did not feel right.

"You don't want to know."

My response silenced her.

After the salon, I wanted to ensure my father wasn't too lonely in that drab nursing home. That was not the only reason. I wanted to be with him, so I drove over before lunch.

"You got your hair cut," he said. He was delighted to see me.

Of his three daughters, I was the only one to wear my hair short.

He noticed what I wore and he was not shy with his opinions. He didn't like my ripped jeans or my trendy jumper-dress with the uneven hem.

About the jumper-dress, he asked, "What's that you're wearing?"

"A very comfortable dress. Why, don't you like it?"

"Not really."

I got a kick out of his straight-forward responses. They made me laugh.

On a previous visit, he said, "You have some grey hair coming in."

"Yes, I know." Amused, I asked, "Do you think I should leave it or colour it?"

He tilted his head to get a closer view and as his open hand waved the air, he said, "Nah…leave it."

Later, I had a chuckle about the conversation with Mel. "I just asked Dad for esthetic advice," and she thought that was pretty funny.

That afternoon at the nursing home, the weather was perfect for an outside visit. My dad sat in his wheelchair and smoked. Being Saturday, the street was busy with people toting bags, pushing strollers, and there were high-end cars and lots of bicycles. It was a dog-friendly hood, which meant every dog that walked by drew my dad's attention.

"There's a good-looking dog."

We talked about breeds and dog training. We discussed food and how my mother became a better cook as she got older. My father had a sweet tooth, and the nursing home offered dessert at lunch and dinner. He told me he had oatmeal for breakfast. A young man had come by to measure him for his own wheelchair. I filled him in about Jack's health and more about the fictional novel I was writing. Close to noon, when I wheeled him toward the dining room, he inquired about Jacquelin's whereabouts.

"I'm not sure, Dad—"

Holding back was hard. In that intimate and private moment, it would have been perfect if I could have told my dad the truth. Mel had been clear about wanting to be with him when he found out about Jacquelin's death. I wanted Mel's support, not only for him, but for me too. But at what cost? At the cost of doing what I often attempted to do in my family—protect others—I held the heavy weight of withholding what my father should know.

***

Back at home in the late afternoon, I turned on my laptop and found the detective's email. A hard set of flutters bounced around in my stomach.

From: C_____ J_____
Date: September 9, 2017 at 1:24 p.m.
Subject: Quote from note…

Beverley,

Hope this helps in the interim. I will look into getting you the original.

It read:

Some lives are not meant to be long, mine is done. I loved music, dance, and business negotiation, flowers esp. roses. I can't face what's coming. I hate my life. It is, and has been for a long time, absolutely pointless. I am free.

I haven't wanted to live for a long time. It is hell. Please don't suffer for me. It is what I want. It's no one's fault but mine. Nothing you could do. Please look after Siron. Any friends I have had and loved, let them know: e.g. "Julianne."

C_____ J_____
Detective #----
XX Division, Toronto Police Service
Criminal Investigation Bureau

I read the email over and over. I studied each paragraph, every sentence, and every single word. I have studied the words and lines more deeply since. Within Jacquelin's articulate words, there were no surprises. She did not address the note to anyone in particular but had to know I would be the only one who ever came to the house. Would she have cared that a police sergeant read it first? I suspect the sergeant passed the note to each detective and likely the coroner too. Had she thought that out? Jacquelin spent hours in front of her computer; research was her thing, and I knew her to be thorough. Did the internet site she visited, "How to Kill Yourself," tell her to consider writing a note and who would likely read it first?

Sitting alone in the heat of the sun coming through the double doors of my upstairs writing room, I felt appreciation for the detective who took time to send me the note. I wrote him back to say thank you. Taking measured breaths, I was aware of the stream of conflicting thoughts trickling in my mind. When the sergeant at the house had said, "there's a note," I felt grateful she took the time to write. So many people who die by suicide, don't leave a note. At least Jacquelin left us with something, I thought. Embarrassingly, I felt pride in her thoughtfulness. Thinking back, where was there room for praise in a heart so full of grief and despair?

I called Mel right away to tell her about the note. I read it to her. I had hoped to talk to her about our sister's final words.

"Send it to me." She sounded angry, so I didn't push our conversation.

I pressed send.

Off the phone, I expectantly waited for the note to appear on the white paper from my printer. I wondered if Mel and I would ever find the right time to talk about the note.

I read Jacquelin's note again and again. Surprised and overwhelmed by its arrival in a mid-afternoon email sent to me by the same detective who was at my dad's house, I was consumed by

Jacquelin's decision to write. For how long had she known what she wanted to say? I was flooded with questions for which there were no answers. I folded the page and placed it in the front flap of my calendar. I go nowhere without my calendar, which meant her final words would always be with me. They would keep my mother's indecipherable words company, as they've been tucked in my wallet since she died four years earlier.

Four
Seven Days in the ICU

December 2013

Usually, my father's voice has a cheerful bounce, but not when he called the morning I was rushing to grade the last of my students' papers before the end-of-semester's deadline.

"Your mother's not eating...She probably has the flu."

"Do you want me to come over?"

"Okay."

I weaved my way through traffic. When I got to their house, my dad was unusually quick to open the door. While he put on the kettle, I wandered into my parents' bedroom. My mother was laying on her back, eyes closed and very, very still.

"Mom. You're not feeling well."

"I'm okay."

"Mom, we need to take you to the doctor."

"Ask him to come here."

My mother liked things to be on her own turf. And she didn't much like doctors, so going out of her way to be with one wasn't going to be easy.

"I'll ask. But if he can't come here, will you go there?"

When I helped her to the washroom, I was shocked by my mother's feebleness. Beneath those baggy fleece pants and turtle necks layered under bulky sweaters existed a woman who was disappearing.

"Yikes, Mom. You're pretty skinny."

In the bathroom, she gazed into the mirror. "I look so old."

My heart sank, "Mom, you're not feeling well."

As her face drooped, she leaned into my body, and we both slid to the floor.

"Dad. Call an ambulance!"

"Mom...stay with me...Dad—she's not breathing. Tell them she stopped breathing!"

It didn't take long before a paramedic came around the corner to find us on the floor. She called out to her colleague and crouched to take a pulse. They brought the stretcher. My father hovered.

"I thought it was the flu," he said.

The paramedic said, "We'll take her into the ambulance and resuscitate her. Then we'll take her to a hospital."

In a few minutes, the second paramedic returned from the driveway to say my mother had regained consciousness.

"We're taking her to Toronto East," she said. "We won't put the siren on because she's no longer in distress. But, if we do, don't panic. Stay calm and drive carefully."

Inside the emergency department, my mom was in a spirited dialogue with the blonde paramedic. I overheard her dispensing wisdom about married life. My dad was listening, too. I liked how the paramedic related to my mother. I think it made her feel good.

The situation changed within seconds. Mom's skin turned grey and my father and I were ushered into the Quiet Room. One of the nurses gently suggested family members should be notified.

"One sister is on a cruise."

"And the other daughter?" The nurse looked into our worried faces. "You don't want any regrets."

"You call her."

"No, Dad. You call her."

The nurse asked, "Is there a problem?"

"Yes, my one sister can be difficult..."

"This is a crisis unit. We're kind of used to it."

But my mother won't like it, I thought. She'll be embarrassed.

My father used the unit's phone to call, and when he did, I heard bargaining from across the room. I could tell she wasn't letting him finish his sentences. Sometimes she did that to me too.

"How'd that go?" I asked.

"Not well."

"Is she coming?"

"We'll have to wait and see."

Among other physical problems, there was a tumour on my mother's ovary. We had to decide: operate or leave the tumor and risk it bursting. According to the surgeon, if the tumour erupted, it could kill her, but so might the operation.

"She's very frail." He was blunt.

Holding out for hope, my father said, "Operate," and I nodded.

The surgery was done close to midnight and we weren't out of there until two o'clock in the morning. Being in the hospital during those quiet hours reminded me of two things: Stephen King's *Shining* and when I had my first MRI at four o'clock in the morning at Toronto Western Hospital. Both examples brought the word 'eerie' to mind.

On the night of my mother's surgery, there was no one else in the waiting room but us—my dad, Jack and Mel's daughter, Marianne and her husband Tim. Mel and Owen were on a cruise ship somewhere warm.

Jacquelin arrived after my mother went into surgery. She was dressed for the cold weather. Over a long puffy-down coat, she wore a grey wool poncho, likely purchased from a consignment shop. Her worn Sorel boots were unlaced with the soiled tongues hanging out. She was lugging a large bag. I had the urge to ask if she'd been to the gym or perhaps was going on a trip. It would have come out sounding sarcastic, so I stayed quiet. As usual, she had an oversized and unzipped purse on her shoulder and a large Tim Hortons cup in her hand.

"How's Mom?"

"We haven't heard anything yet."

The waiting room was lined with built-in benches covered in vinyl. I liked being able to face one another. The five of us were close enough to talk without raising our voices, which was a relief because that would have been exhausting.

There was room for Jacquelin, but she didn't sit with us. With all of her stuff, she went to the opposite side of the room.

She seemed too alone and that made me feel helpless and sad.

While waiting for the surgeon, there was little else to do but watch Jacquelin root through her stuff. I noticed Marianne and Tim's eyes growing wider, checking-in with one another. My dad glanced over every once in a while, but mostly he looked at the floor and checked his watch a lot.

I broke the silence. "How are you doing, Jacq?"

"I'm fine." A too-quick response.

She drank from her cup.

"How did you get here?" I asked.

She took a swig.

"Cab."

Jacquelin as her previous self—six or seven years earlier— took pride in how she presented to the world. Her laces would be tied and the smart-looking coat would have been in good repair. On the night of my mother's surgery, Jacquelin was getting close to becoming unrecognizable.

While my family nestled in the corner of the waiting area a loud voice came out of nowhere.

"It's just another asshole calling. It's just another asshole calling."

My chest tightened. I looked to see Jacquelin fumbling through the over-filled purse. Marianne's eyes had grown wider, and I had to suppress a laugh. I may have been exhausted. My dad's eyes rose from the floor. I could see the muted smile on Tim's face, and Jack's eyebrows were knitted.

"Just another asshole calling. Just another asshole…" repeated Jacquelin's ring tone.

Relieved we had the room to ourselves, I whispered, "Mom would hate this."

"You're not kidding," said my dad.

Jacquelin finally found the phone. "Hi…yep…at the hospital…" Her words were clipped. "No. …. Yeah…talk to you late—NO!…I CAN'T…. What the fuck? What's wrong with you anyway? I SAID NO. …No…. Nope…. Okay. Ciao."

She fiddled with the phone and I wondered if she was blocking the caller. That's what I would have done.

Unable to resist, and in his driest tone, my dad asked, "Who was that you were talking to, Jacquelin?"

"A friend." Translation: "Mind your own business."

"Oh." The familiar mockery in his abbreviated response gave me a giggle.

Within minutes, more noise. It had to be Jacquelin's phone because my dad didn't have one and everyone else was following the rules. We had read the sign: "CELL PHONE USE FORBIDDEN."

Sure enough, ring tones of flutes and trumpets came from the purse.

"Hi…Yeah…No, the doctor hasn't come out yet."

She was civil—evidently, she wasn't talking to the other asshole.

About an hour later, the surgeon and nurse entered the room. Their scrubs were rumpled and their heads were sweaty. The surgeon was pleased with how things had gone. My mother's tumor was on its way to pathology.

I cringed when Jacquelin stood and walked toward the surgeon and nurse.

Even-tempered and respectful, her questions were informed, while she presented them with a range of propositions. I was nervous as hell.

An affirming nod from the surgeon confirmed Jacquelin's medical-pharmaceutical knowledge.

"You've done your homework," he said.

I thought she was showing off.

"My friend was a doctor in the Iranian military..."

Jacquelin's doctor friend lived in her basement. According to her, he suffered from PTSD—Post Traumatic Stress Disorder. She'd met him at an AA meeting. After one year of sobriety, he was back on the booze. So was she. I suspected they were lovers.

"Well, your friend is right," said the surgeon.

They talked some more, and I hoped her obnoxious phone wouldn't go off again.

Beaming with admiration, my dad leaned in. "She really knows what's she talking about."

"Hmmm."

After the medical team left, I felt the need to check in with everyone.

"What do you think, Dad?"

"Sounds like things went pretty well."

"Yes..."

Jacquelin gathered her bags and layered on clothes— coat, scarf and poncho. She swung the heavy bag onto her shoulder.

"Jacq. We'll drive you home."

"Already called a cab." Translation: "Leave me the hell alone."

She walked through the automatic doors the same way she came in—weighed down in clothes that didn't look like they were really hers. Besides keeping her warm on a cold winter's night, the layered clothes were her new protection, I thought. She was no longer glamorous, not even for a budding bag lady.

I felt helpless watching her walk down the stark, white hallway alone. I held her in my sights until the doors closed and blocked my view.

***

When Mel and Owen got back from their trip, Marianne brought her mother up to speed. She chastised her for not leaving any contact information. Jet-lagged, Mel joined us in the ICU. My mother, who referred to Mel and Owen's holidays as "gallivanting" and "a waste of money," cast Mel dismissive glances. Was she still angry at Mel for going away? The tension was palpable.

That's why I buoyed my voice to say, "Mom, your traveler is back." Instead of telling me to "cut the bullshit," like she sometimes did, my mother smiled, and Mel was forgiven.

***

A week after her operation, the doctor suggested to Dad and Mel that it was time to bring the family together.

When Mel's number came up on my phone I pulled to the side of the road.

"Bev, you need to come back."

"Okay. It'll take me about fifteen minutes."

"That's okay. Drive carefully."

"I will. Have you called Jacq?"

"No not yet. Gonna do that now."

I returned to the ICU and heard Mel on the phone.

"Jacq, I'm not making this up. Please. It would be a really good idea if you came."

Jacquelin must have responded loudly, because Mel held the phone away from her ear.

"Jacquelin, listen to me…the doctors don't think Mom is going to last much longer. So, you need to come."

It was clear Jacquelin was being combative.

"No…No…Jacq…she's really uncomfortable and she's having trouble breathing." After a few more seconds of frustrated listening, Mel added, "I have to tell you that Mom has asked to be taken off of life-support, Jacquelin, and I'm trying to tell you that the doctors are saying she's not going to last much longer."

Pacing back and forth while looking at me with pleading eyes, Mel said, "Yes, Bev's here and so is Dad. You need to be here too. Jacq, get here as soon as you can."

When Mel hung up the phone, I asked, "Is she coming?"

"I'm not sure."

"Where is she?"

"She didn't say."

"What did she say at the end?" I asked.

"She told me to go fuck myself."

Without another word we put the drama behind us and attended to our mother. My father sat beside Mom with his hand on her arm. When he spoke to her, he called her Jackie, the name he used when he was feeling most tender.

"Jackie, the doctors told us that you don't want to live anymore. Do you really want to go?"

She closed her eyes and nodded.

He paused to look at me and asked her again, "Jackie, you don't want to live anymore?"

She shook her head. "No."

My father's blue eyes grew misty.

I said, "Mom, does this mean you want to say 'goodbye?'"

As the palliative nurse looked on, my mother nodded.

Our eyes filled with tears as machines purred in the background.

"Oh Jackie," said my dad, "I'm sure gonna miss you. We've had a good long life together."

She smiled and nodded.

Holding her hand to his lips, he said, "I love you, Jackie. I'll see you on the other side."

She mouthed, "I love you, too."

Taking her hand next, I said, "Mom, we'll take care of Dad."

She moved her head from side to side, "No." I took that to mean she wanted him to take care of himself. Just a few days earlier, when she could still speak, she told him to get out of the wheelchair. "You should be walking." She was right.

"Okay, Mom, I get it. But we'll visit him a lot."

Mel placed her hand on my mother's arm. "I love you, Mom."

She spoke with her lips, "I love you, too."

"I'll watch over Jacquelin the best way I can," I said.

My mother shrugged. Did she regret not knowing what more to do for Jacquelin? Was she expressing defeat? Or something else? Her hands lifted to the ceiling. Was she gesturing toward heaven? Had she surrendered and turned her youngest daughter's struggles over to God? My mom wasn't religious or expressive about God. If she prayed, she was private about it.

I wondered if she was telling me to let go.

It was my turn: "Mom," my voice cracked, "I love you."

Her lips told me that she loved me too, and, in that moment, I never felt closer to my mother.

With my dad on one side and Mel and I on the other, her eyes closed, and she squeezed our hands for the very last time. My mother took her last breath with her family—everyone except Jacquelin.

Equipment was discretely turned off and anything portable was wheeled out of the room. The palliative-care nurse hovered respectfully. I stayed at mom's side, and my dad sat in a wheelchair opposite me, still holding her hand. Mel stood at the end of the bed and we held our silent vigil. Silent that is, until Jacquelin entered into the room holding a Tim Horton's coffee cup in one hand and her oversized bag in the other. She was wearing another poncho over her coat.

"What's happening?"

Mel was the first to speak. "She's gone, Jacq."

"She died?"

"Yes."

She moved to my mother's side. Gently, she brushed my mother's bangs to one side. "I was here last night and she was fine."

Mel said, "Well, that's not what the doctors said. Mom had a hard night."

"Oh! So they decided to kill her?"

I chose my words carefully. "Jacquelin, that's not what happened. Mom has been suffering and she made a choice."

The nurse had quietly slipped away and returned with Dr. Warren, head physician in the ICU. When he introduced himself to Jacquelin, she glared at him.

"Dr. Warren," I said, "maybe you could tell my sister how things went."

With compassion and grace, he explained the details of my mother's failing organs.

"She had an inability to breathe on her own or take any food or communicate with her family…essentially, she'd be machine dependent for the rest of her life…and from what your mother told me, she didn't want to live her life like that."

"She didn't want to be here," barked Jacquelin. "She hated doctors and hospitals. Didn't trust them. Never has."

He didn't miss a beat. "All the more reason for your mother to have made the decision she did. We knew when your mother came in here seven days ago, she wouldn't be leaving. There was a lot going on and it was too much for her body to bear."

Jacquelin picked up her bag and walked out of the room with her Tim Hortons cup in hand.

Earlier, I learned from the ICU nurse that Jacquelin had been visiting "at very late hours." I didn't think visiting in the middle of the night was the best thing for Jacquelin. I wanted to trust my mother got some comfort in her youngest daughter's visits. At the very least, my mother wasn't alone in a place she never wanted to be.

Mel had been clear, "Mom's not going to last much longer," but Jacquelin didn't listen. She often said our mother was her best friend. I wondered how she felt about missing her mother's last living moments. Did she regret taking the time to stand in the lineup for a Tim Hortons coffee?

The next time I saw her was at the funeral home to pick out the casket. She didn't approve of our dad's choice of a plain casket and when he scoffed at the cost of the flowers, she reminded him about his frugality. Mel and I agreed, and everyone laughed. It was a moment of sister-solidarity.

Due to the huge ice storm and power outage across the province, the date for my mother's funeral was changed three times. Dogs included, everyone in the family except Jacquelin found refuge at our place, because our neighbourhood got its power back first. Having my family close reminded me of weekends at the cottage. It was a good feeling.

Five days after my mother's death, I prepared Christmas dinner and everyone was invited. Jacquelin did not show up. The focus was on my father but Mel and I shared worries about Jacquelin.

"She's probably at Boy Toy's, which might be okay because the guy doesn't drink—"

Overhearing us, Jack said, "Yeah but he's a whack-job in every other way."

Like sisters sometimes do, Mel and I groaned in unison. We both knew that Jacquelin met Howie, whom I call Boy Toy, on a dating website. Soon after, she told me he carried a sexual assault charge.

"Jacquelin, not a good idea…move on…"

"He's says the woman was just a revengeful bitch."

She dismissed my words of caution. When Mel tried talking to her, she was told to "butt out."

Eventually he was incarcerated and she was back on the booze, struggling not to drink. It didn't help that she was visiting him at the institution. His family had encouraged the visits, and his father, whom she liked very much, drove her there. Eventually Jacquelin confided in me about the strain of those visits.

"I get it, Jacq, his family has been good to you but right now they're looking out for their son. Seeing Howie in jail isn't good for you. Anyone would find that hard."

Mel never met Boy Toy, but Jack and I did. One time he loitered outside an AA meeting we went to with Jacquelin. After the meeting I was pleased to see her networking with a few AA women on the church steps. In my mind, if the AA community became her refuge, I could step away. When I glanced across the street and saw Boy Toy's vehicle, with his arm swinging out the window, my heart sank. His body language screamed impatience and when Jacquelin saw him, she cut her conversation with the women short.

Watching too, Jack was disgusted. "That little prick needs to leave her the hell alone."

Not disagreeing, I stayed quiet until the next conversation with my sister.

Five
Another Diagnosis

January 1, 2014

Mel, Owen and Jack and I spent a quiet New Year's Eve at Dad's house. It was low-key until a few minutes after midnight when Jack announced we needed to go to the hospital.

"What for?"

"I coughed up blood. We gotta go."

No one in the room missed the panic in his voice.

Mel said, "Go, go Bev. Call us later."

Jack and I spent the early hours of New Year's Day, 2014, in the same hospital where my mother had died eleven days earlier. The doctor who examined Jack described three reasons people cough up blood. Cancer was one of them. Eight months later Jack's first oncologist found a small spot in the lower lobe of his left lung and, in August, 2014, Jack had a lobectomy. One-half of his left lung was removed.

When it was time to bring him home from the hospital, I overheard Jack telling the nurse he didn't feel ready to leave. He had two pigtail tubes with Pneumostat chest drain valves attached to them, draining the wound. The incision where the lung was sutured had come apart. He said he didn't feel well and, from his strained face, I knew he was frightened.

We were given two syringes and dozens of alcohol swabs and the nurse gave us a quick demonstration on how to empty the Pneumostat. We were told to expect a call from Community Care Nursing to arrange daily nurse visits.

That night, Alexander, the nurse, emptied the Pneumostat and checked the tubes. The next night, another nurse redressed the wounds and emptied the Pneumostat. Our third nurse checked Jack's blood pressure and asked if he had an irregular heartbeat.

"No, not that we know of."

In the same nurse's following visit, I reported Jack's complaint about feeling chilled. She blamed "the stupid drugs."

"Hmmm…"

As soon as she left, I called the surgeon's secretary to report on Jack's fever. In the hospital's outpatient department at seven o'clock the next morning, we heard Dr. Lue had been called into emergency surgery. We waited. Jack was sore, withdrawn, and when he did speak, grumpy. The head nurse expressed embarrassment about the long wait. Eventually, one of the resident doctors became convinced there was an infection. Each time he touched the wound, even with tender care, Jack screeched profanities.

"Sorry," whispered the flush-faced resident.

"Yeah well, it hurts!"

I cringed.

Wincing, the resident said, "I'm sorry but the tubes have to come out."

With each tug at every small stitch securing the plastic tube inside his body, Jack screamed the f-word. Helpless, I could only watch from the side. I held my breath a lot. The stressed resident was swearing too, but not so loudly.

"Almost done…hold on, Jack… I know this is hard…just try to hold on…breathe…"

Three feet of tubing were removed from Jack's first wound. There was a second wound, also infected. Jack and the resident braced themselves to tackle the task. With an infection, and no local anaesthetic, the pain was excruciating. Thankfully, no one came to complain about the profanities.

Dr. Lue arrived from his other emergency, and apologies were genuinely expressed and accepted. Appearing displeased, the surgeon proceeded to remove all of the gauze and tape that his resident had methodically placed around the wounds. He told Jack new tubes would be inserted and he arranged for X-rays and CT-scans.

"You need to be readmitted." Dr. Lue was going on vacation and rather than leaving him in the care of his residents he wanted to send us back to East York General, under the watchful eye of his trusted colleague.

In the office of Dr. Simone, less than an hour later, the second set of tubes was removed. I don't recall his reasoning. Once again, no anaesthetic and a lot more screaming laced with profanities. Unlike the resident, Dr. Simone didn't once wince.

When the surgeon said Jack could go home, I couldn't have felt more certain about that being a bad idea. From behind Jack's chair, I looked Dr. Simone in the eye and shook my head.

"On second thought, we'll admit you. It's after-hours…You'll need to get admitted through the emergency department."

We knew what that meant.

"You've got to be kidding." Jack was loud and abrupt.

"No, I'm not," said the surgeon. His voice was curt.

I squeezed Jack's shoulder. "It's okay. Thank you, Doctor."

At the elevator Jack muttered, "I really don't like that guy."

"Shush, I know."

Since arriving in Dr. Simone's office on that Friday afternoon, the hospital had become quiet. I pushed Jack, sitting in the abandoned wheelchair I had found, through the hushed corridors. Four hours later, Jack was in a hospital bed. The infection worsened and he remained there for twenty-five more days.

It was the first time I thought I was going to lose him.

Six

An Unresolved Dance with Suicide Loss

Summer, 1980

In July of 1980 when I was twenty-two and freshly divorced from my first husband, my colleague Mary assumed I was lonely and invited me to dinner. She also invited Greg, her husband's younger brother. Appetizers were served by the pool, and Mary's husband Glen prepared the barbecue. An evening with Mary, in Glen and Greg's company, was like meeting her for the first time. She was playful and carefree and not once did she quote scripture like how she sometimes did in the classroom where we co-taught. (I felt quite irritated when she did that.)

Greg, was single and exceedingly quiet, not at all like Mary's gregarious husband. In a whispered conversation in her kitchen, she said she could tell Greg liked me. According to Mary, Greg would like to have a girlfriend.

"H-he seems like a nice guy." The idea of meeting a nice guy gave me the jitters and discomfort set in. I had hoped the evening at Mary's would be one of levity and laughter. It wasn't.

When the phone rang, Glen said, "Mary, we have company, let it go to the machine."

Too late. "Hello?...Oh Shirley...hello—"

She held the phone to her ear and turned in my direction. She mouthed, "It's Shirley...Joe's mother..."

I was surprised a parent of one of our adult students would call Mary at her home.

With her hand over the receiver, Mary said, "She's really upset...Joe threatened to kill himself."

Twenty-year-old Joe had been referred to our life skills job readiness program by his employment counsellor. From the day he started, he evoked laughter in his peers, me included. At the time of his mother's call, he was already in week-eight of the sixteen-week program. The program included one-on-one counselling, and Mary and I had divided the list of student names into two. Joe was Mary's client.

When she spoke to Shirley, Mary said, "Bev's here too...She and I will talk and call you right back."

Mary planted herself on the sofa beside her husband and looked at me from across the room.

"The woman's beside herself. One of us needs to go over there. Talk him down—"

Without thinking the matter through, my young twenty-two-year-old-life-skills-coach-naïve-self jumped at the opportunity to help. I hadn't thought to call one of my esteemed mentors. Nor did it occur to either of us, that Mary and I should go together. She was not my boss, but there was no question she had more experience than me and, in my mind, more authority and know-how.

"I can do it," I said.

When I think back, I wonder if my exuberance to rescue Joe had been provoked by the detail Mary whispered to me in her kitchen. Too bad she drew my attention to Greg's romantic interest in me. Had she not, I probably would not have noticed. I was too busy pretending not to be suffering from my ex-husband's infidelities during our brief marriage. My battered ego and broken heart left me numb. My remedy was to keep moving. I had been residing in a whirlwind of change. We had sold our house, I bought a new car and for my new teaching position, I moved out of the city. Instead of staying in one place to think, I had the constant urge to be on the move. I took up running and cycled long distances. I drove too fast between Niagara and Toronto and when I lurched from place to place I was accused of seeking a geographic cure. Mary's invitation to dinner was her attempt to reach out and fill the gap and that might have worked for the evening had Greg's tenderness not incited me to bolt. I did not want to be with a kind man who might have liked me in a way more than I could handle. Shirley's phone call was my escape hatch.

Outside her front door, Mary placed her hand on my shoulder and laughed. "You almost got dessert."

"Yeah—"

"Thank you for this. I'd do it, but with Greg here, it's best you go. You'll be great."

Embracing my seasoned colleague's endorsement without question, I hopped into my car and drove out of her neighbourhood.

Joe and his mother Shirley were the first people I knew to have tragically lost a family member to death by suicide. I arrived at their bungalow and found mother and son standing side by side in the garage. From what Joe had shared early on with the group, I knew that was where his father had died. In the group, he never mentioned suicide. He had said that his father died "suddenly."

When I got there Shirley said Joe was distraught and she was afraid he would take his own life like his father had.

"I thought the program was helping him," she sobbed.

"It is. He was doing well—" At least I thought he was.

"He speaks so highly of Mary. I didn't know who else to call. He talks about you too, so I'm glad you could come."

Before turning to Joe, I told her she had done the right thing.

"Joe, let's go for a walk."

"No."

His mother urged him to listen to me. "Bev's come all this way—"

He yanked his arm away from her reach. "I said, no."

"How about a drive, then?" I looked at his mother, "Shirley, want to come for a drive?"

She shook her head. Without saying anything, Joe opened the car door and got into the passenger seat.

Shirley, appearing worn out, waited while I backed out of her driveway. To indicate I had matters handled, I gave her a quick wave and headed out of their street. I didn't know the area well, so I drove in the direction of the college. I parked on the quiet road behind the college parking lot.

"Ready to talk?"

"No." He sounded like a petulant teenager.

Reaching for the right words, I said, "I can see you're upset—"

"I'm fine."

He asked if he could turn on the radio.

"Y-yeah, sure," I said.

He found the station he wanted—country—and leaned back and shut his eyes. I waited, and when he finally said something, I turned down the radio.

"I didn't get along with my old man," he began. They fought a lot, he said. "Sometimes it got physical."

Joe said his mother lied to the insurance company about how his father had died. "Otherwise, she wouldn't have been able to get any money," he added.

It was tough making sense of everything that spluttered from his mouth. I didn't interrupt and I knew he had to find someone, other than me, to talk to. He needed to talk to a professional who knew about suicide.

We sat in the dark for a long time. He cried and yelled, and when he started to make tasteless jokes about death and suicide, I said, "Joe, it's getting late. I need to get back."

"Take me to my sister's. I don't want to be with my mother right now." His abrupt demand didn't go unnoticed.

At his sister's, we were greeted in the driveway. I pulled on the handbrake, Joe got out, and slammed the door harder than I liked. He pushed by his sister.

She ignored him. "You must be Bev. My mom called and said you'd probably bring him here. Come in."

"Okay…but just for a few minutes."

Their spacious flat was on the second floor of an adorable old country house.

"Coffee?"

To be polite, I said "Yes, thank you. Just half a cup, please."

After water boiled on the stove, she poured it over instant crystals into two mugs. Before joining her husband on the couch, she retrieved him a beer from the fridge. No one offered Joe anything to drink. I thought that strange.

I sat on a small wooden chair and listened to two siblings and an in-law talk about Shirley's deceased husband. According to them, he had been depressed but it never occurred to anyone he would "kill himself."

"He took the coward's way out," snarled the brother-in-law.

Joe's sister said, "It was a selfish thing to do."

The couple agreed on the impact of the shock.

"It's been hell for my mother-in-law." The brother-in-law took a swig of beer. "She's the one who found him. Don't think she'll ever get over it."

I nodded and tried to imagine her turmoil. "It must have been horrible." I wondered how someone gets over the bleakness of such a horrible ending. I'd heard some people consider suicide a violent act.

I knew so little about suicide then I wasn't sure how to talk about it. When I joined in on their conversation, I navigated my choice of words. I remembered when Emile Durkheim's book *Suicide* was assigned in my first-year sociology class; I had not anticipated its future relevance to my life. Too bad I hadn't read it more closely. I didn't think suicide would come anywhere close to me.

Eight years later, in 1988, when I taught in the social service worker program, I did come to a fuller understanding on the topic after inviting social-activist Karen Letofsky to my classroom. Karen introduced us to the Toronto Distress Centre and the controversial proposal to construct the Luminous Veil along both sides of the Bloor Street Viaduct—also known as the Prince Edward Viaduct—for the purpose of deterring suicide by jumping. At the time, the location, known as a "suicide magnet," was the second most used bridge for suicide in the world.

The whole time while in his sister's flat, Joe uttered very few words, except to grumble something negative about the mess his father had left. He mostly glared at the floor. I suspected this was how he grieved. Was he still in shock? Was the conversation in the room too much to take in? Was he feeling guilty about some of the unkind things he had said about his deceased father? He resembled none of the features of the comical carefree person he presented in the life skills group.

Turning my attention to Joe's sister and her husband, I said, "It's so good you're talking about this." I got up from the chair. "I should be going—"

Joe scrambled to his feet.

"No. Stay," he yelped. I was right, the easy-going man I'd met eight weeks ago, the one who made me laugh, was no longer in the room.

"Joe," I said softly, hoping he'd understand, "I have to teach in the morning. It's late."

"Stay longer."

Clear about what I needed—sleep—and a break from the family's intensity, I stood my ground, "No. I have to go."

I thanked his sister for the coffee and walked toward the door. Joe grabbed my arm and, without any warning, flung me across the wooden floor. I slid and landed against the fridge. Aghast and bewildered, I gawked at his sister and brother-in-law. They looked away. Holy shit, I thought, how the hell did I get myself into this situation? Their idleness spoke volumes: Joe had done this before. That's when I knew I was alone in finding a safe way out.

I had a plan. First, I had to get out of the flat, and then down the narrow steep wooden stairs. There were at least fifty of them. I was convinced Joe wasn't thinking straight and I feared what he could be capable of— being pushed down the stairs was top of mind. Running toward the door was out of the question and, since no one was listening, so was screaming.

I stayed calm. "Joe, we can talk tomorrow."

"You're lying to me," he growled.

Doing my best to be brave, I stepped closer to the door.

"I'm not lying." Yes, I was. Call it lying or negotiation, but I was not telling him the truth.

On the tiny platform at the top of the stairs, his presence bothered me. For assurance, I held onto the banister.

He smelled my fear. "Hey, you're not so smart after all, eh?"

On each step, Joe inched behind me, so to feel safe, I kept reassuring him I'd see him the next day. Lies, lies and more lies. Outside, on flat ground, I was thankful for the moist night air on my face. My little red Honda was a few steps away, and I knew I wouldn't feel safe until I got inside and drove away. I opened the door and kept talking. I slid into the driver's seat, and when I saw anger in his eyes, I knew I'd done well to get away.

The next day in the group I did not see Joe. But in the early evening I looked out to see three men in a beat-up vehicle parked beneath the window of my second-floor flat. I heard Joe tell his buddies to wait. He climbed the stairs nosily and knocked on the feeble door.

"Bev, I know you're in there…I'm really sorry…I promise I'll never do that again…I was just upset…"

He banged harder, and I stayed crunched on the floor. I didn't respond. Trembling, I tried my best to breathe in silence. How he had grabbed my arm and tossed me across the room left me with no question about his physical strength. My worst fear was that he'd knock the door down.

Joe gave up banging and when he climbed into the back seat of his friend's vehicle and slammed the door, the driver gunned the engine before driving away.

Minutes later, my neighbour Christopher tapped on the door.

"Bev, it's me, Chris. You okay in there?"

I opened the door. "Yes. I'm okay."

"What the hell was that?"

I don't recall all of what I told Chris.

"You look like you need to get out the hell outta here…Let's go to Buffalo. Get something to eat and find some music."

Chris, like me, was in an in-between time in his life. His marriage had come to an unhappy end but the person he missed the most was his daughter. When she visited, he sometimes included me.

He loved blues and he knew where to find it in Buffalo's darkest venues, including someone's back-lane garage. At one-thirty in the morning, the small crowd moaned with pleasure when Muddy Waters strolled into the yard with his electric guitar. Word about the gig must have gotten out because the people kept coming and more tables and fold-up chairs were added. Chris retrieved beers from the cooler underneath the table and he threw a few dollars into the hat. It didn't take long for Waters's sultry music to seep into my soul.

Waters sang, "Well, now, there's two, there's two trains running, Well, they ain't never, no, going my way."

Stepping into an underground culture of music with Chris at my side tempered what had happened earlier in the evening with Joe. I was submerged between rustic sounds and my teaching day, which was just a few hours away.

At the inception of my teaching life when Joe was among the first of my students, I knew little about the topic of suicide. However, I intuitively understood the kind of power Joe attempted to exert over me. When he had come to my flat, I had no intention of giving him a second chance. He scared me, and thank goodness I did not open the door. I don't think Joe formally withdrew from the program—students who fled, seldom did. In her role as his primary counsellor, Mary spoke to the worker who referred him to our program, and hopefully he was able to help Joe to move forward in his unresolved grief about his father's suicide.

Joe is a part of my story that I continue to draw on to encourage women—students and friends—who are confronted with violence by the people they thought were okay. With conviction, I have told them to walk away. In my professional life, I also made note to keep all interactions with any student inside the boundaries of worktime. My encounter with Joe was a raw experience about professional boundaries, something else I would later tell my students.

Did fourteen-year-old Jacquelin know that her oldest sister had been thrown across the hardwood floor and been fearful enough the next day that she crouched in the corner of her bedroom so an enraged man could not hear her breath?

Did Jacquelin ever become one of the women I encouraged to walk away at the first sniff of physical or emotional abuse? Yes. I was not explicit about my encounter with Joe, but my brief entanglement with his bad temper and unresolved anger and the danger it put me in, informed me about where Jacquelin could be heading when she stepped into dark places with sordid people. From Boy Toy Howie, I had heard reports of men other than himself, who had physically pushed my sister around. When I spoke to Jacquelin about this, she told me he was lying. I wasn't so sure. I suspect Jacquelin faked being street smart in the same way I pretended to be brave. I knew that her apparent fearlessness was fueled by alcohol and that was one of the reasons I could not trust her to walk alone in the dark.

Seven
Help Came My Way

September 8, 2017

Friday 9:30 a.m.

A woman from Toronto's Victim Services called within thirty-six hours of my discovering Jacquelin had taken her own life. The voice on the other end of the phone said the police had passed along the details of my sister's suicide.

"You've been through something horrific." Her gentleness gave me the sense she understood the depth of my loss. She encouraged me not to underestimate the impact of encountering my youngest sister in the way I did.

Tears welled in my throat. "I'm still trying to make sense of everything."

"That's understandable. It will take some time to come to terms with what you saw. You've experienced a trauma… You are likely still in shock…"

I felt numb. The timing of the call could not have been better. She introduced herself but unfortunately, my head was too full to retain her name. She listened through my lack of clarity and tears. I don't recall everything she said but I remember her tender warning about expecting some days to be harder than others. I later came to know this. She said it was important to talk about what happened. She urged me not to go through the next days, weeks and months, alone. The woman encouraged me to contact Alex, the person who ran Toronto's Distress and Crisis Centre. I had no intention of going through my complicated and insurmountable grief alone.

I called the number right away.

"You've done an important thing." Alex's calmness helped to settle my stomach.

He asked how I was doing. "Have you had any thoughts of personal self-harm?"

I recall the essence of his question and I understood the reason. When I later went to the Harvard Health website, I found his question mirrored there.

People who've recently lost someone to suicide are at an increased risk for thinking about, planning, or attempting suicide. After any loss of a loved one, it's not unusual to wish you were dead; that doesn't mean you'll act on the wish. But if these feelings persist or grow more intense.... (www.health.harvard.edu.com)

"No," I said, "I am not going to hurt myself." I was just extremely sad and I knew I needed to get help if I was going to survive my jittery emotions.

He told me about the drop-in groups he ran in an office space above the North York Plaza and another one in Trinity Square behind the Eaton Centre. The earliest drop-in was scheduled for the upcoming Monday at seven-thirty in the evening.

The sooner the better, I thought. "I'll come to the one at Trinity Square, and my husband will be with me."

"That would be fine."

On Monday evening Jack and I took the creaky stairs one floor up to a landing outside an office with a frosted-glass door. There was no place to sit on the landing where we waited outside his office and nothing to look at on the wall, so I leaned my tired body against it. When more people arrived, an awkward silence trailed whispered hellos and furtive glances. The longer we waited the less sure I felt about being among strangers in an old musty house on a hot September night. I stepped closer to Jack.

Looking older than his years, Alex shuffled from his office, and we six people who had been huddled, waiting together in the hallway, followed him into a room that at earlier time was likely someone's bedroom. There was no air conditioning and the room smelled stale. Thankfully, Alex opened the window. He organized chairs into a circle and I sat beside a young attractive woman with long blonde hair. Jack was between me and another woman. She had also come alone. I detected a Mexican accent and I thought of John, Jacquelin's ex-husband. Across from me was a man and woman in their early forties who told us they were long-time Canadians who were born in Trinidad.

Everyone in the room, including Alex, had lost a loved one to suicide: a younger sister, a boyfriend, an uncle and a cousin. I noticed as many differences among our shared stories as there were similarities. No one escaped shock, despair and unanswered questions. We were at varying places in the web of grief. The blonde woman sobbed through the whole session. She and her boyfriend had argued, and soon after, he took his life in the park under their favourite tree. She had found him on Sunday night, fewer than twenty-four hours before sitting in the chair beside me. I sensed she was falling apart, and her fragile and raw state reminded me of myself a few days earlier when I found Jacquelin. She blamed herself. After mindful listening, Alex invited her to stay behind so they could talk. His offer filled me with relief. The woman beside Jack was bewildered and upset by her family's harsh and unsympathetic reaction to her much-loved cousin's death. They accused the deceased cousin of being sinful. She talked about how hard it was to be so far away from Mexico where her cousin went to vacation and then take her life. When the quiet husband of the married couple reached for words to describe his uncle, his boisterous wife finished his sentences. I was relieved Alex noticed and gently encouraged each of us to take as much time as we needed to sort through our thoughts. Jack talked a little bit about how he saw Jacquelin struggle in the last few years of her life and how hard it was to helplessly watch. When I shared, I talked about sometimes treating my sister like my daughter, and Alex said his story about his sister was similar to mine.

I told the group how clean and tidy I found the house on the night of Jacquelin's suicide.

Alex looked into my face and nodded. "She was preparing."

I nodded. "Yes. I was wondering about that." I wrapped my arms around my stomach and Jack put his warm hand on my back.

Through empathy and his ability to hear beyond our words, Alex facilitated the conversation toward self-care and the days ahead and our own mental health. He repeated that a suicide is more complicated and traumatic than grieving other losses. He said it can be hard to find a safe place to talk about this taboo subject. He said people don't always know how to help or what to say. Besides being sudden, suicide is usually unexpected, and when police and coroners are involved it all adds to the cold feeling of being overwhelmed.

Most of what he said resonated with me deeply. In regard to the idea of unexpectedness, I remembered that the notion of Jacquelin ending her life had crossed my mind in the past, and when it did, I had checked in with her about it. A 2016 journal entry showed that I planned to double up on my prayers for her.

She's so unhappy, distressed and on the edge. I was on the edge too. *She worries me. I don't think she will kill herself, but I don't think she wants to live.* She told me, "I dug a deep hole." *Her life is dark. Her life painful. But she keeps digging. She doesn't listen. It appears she has no faith. Sounds like this job is on the skids.*

In the drop-in group a couple of people nodded when Alex said we might find ourselves experiencing stigma, shame or isolation. Shame never entered my mind, because that's not how I have ever thought about suicide. I remembered someone had asked me if I felt guilty about Jacquelin's death, and my answer to him was "no." My feelings of responsibility for her never felt wrong. I believed I had done all I could do to keep my sister afloat, so the feeling of guilt had not been stirred. However, it was early and I knew well enough I could surprise myself.

The topic of mental illness and addiction came up in the circle. Even before her death I was uncertain if Jacquelin was a victim of mental illness. Her sudden bout of alcoholism was real, and I was unclear if they were one and the same. Was she self-medicating? Some thought so. Maybe she died by suicide because she could no longer cope with how she saw her circumstances—intolerable. Maybe she was worn out. Unanswered questions.

A few days earlier at my sister's funeral, I had told Roman, a long-time friend who had tried to support Jacquelin in finding a sober life, that mental illness was her struggle and likely the reason for her death.

Roman shook his head and didn't mince his words, "Bev, it was the alcohol, and an army of people tried to help her."

Johnny nodded. He was someone Jacquelin had trusted, and on more than one occasion I reached out to him for help. Sometimes when I didn't know where Jacquelin was, Johnny did. If he told me she was at an AA meeting or that he had spoken to her on the phone, my heart would get lighter. But almost always during those conversations, just like Roman used to say, Johnny had also said, "She's not ready."

The book Alcoholics Anonymous, commonly called The Big Book, had been among Jacquelin's belongings I had kept. Without giving it a close look, I placed it on my book shelf. Five years later, I picked it up and flipped through the pages for the first time and that's when I saw what was written inside the cover.

"A gift from my sister-in-law who did not make it out alive—<u>learn from this</u>."

It was Jack's writing and he had underlined the last three words. Finding Jack's penciled inscription five years after Jacquelin's death caused my heart to skip. He has known many people who have not survived their fight with alcohol and now my youngest sister was one of them. The words in Jack's inscription were as clear as the strength behind Roman's words and Johnny's affirming nod. Emotionally shaken, I carried the book to the couch and flipped through the pages. At first glance the book looked pristine. But on page eight random words were circled. Over on page seventy-five was an underlining that made me wonder what sense Jacquelin made about fears falling away in perfect peace and ease. Did she ever get close to feeling such peace? As I read on, I pictured Jacquelin contemplating about what it meant to feel nearer to God. From the loopy writing I could tell it was Jacquelin who also circled a phrase about how dark it can be before the sun rises.

When I told a long-time member of AA about all of the circles Jacquelin had put around the word "resentment," he offered a warm smile.

"Resentment is the number one defect of character that causes most alcoholics to return to drinking."

His response aligned with how I saw Jacquelin. Her tone got sharper over time, and when she moved into my father's house, her mood grew gloomier. She never seemed helpful and was always angry. During those times I found it harder to reach her. I had been witnessing my sister's self-esteem dwindle. I thought of "resentment" as her enemy. Alcohol changed her.

In an earlier journal entry, I wrote:

I feel like Jacquelin is my whole life right now. I don't like it. I try to go about my business – writing, church stuff, dog walking, exercise classes, cooking – but my mind still fills with her. When I wake, she's there. She's in my dreams too. Almost every conversation with Jack, who has more than enough on his plate, I have to resist talking about my sister. Questions to self: am I over-involved? do I have attachment issues? how would anyone else experience a similar situation? Answers: none yet but chanting the slogan, "Let go and let God," sometimes helps. Another

question: how to let go? Thinking: I trust God. I'm one of those people who feels her prayers are heard. I feel good about that. I've been patient for answers. Waiting works. I have asked for help and guidance. So, I have to remind myself to keep leaning into my faith. Maybe I'm already doing what I'm supposed to be doing. Ah…thank you journal.
      `[Journal entry, February 4, 2016]

Jacquelin introduced me to Leonard Cohen's *Anthem*, a 1992 album, in which he sang about "the light getting in through the crack." When she was drinking hard, she left little space for people or their light to slip through the cracks. How I wish she had returned to singing the lyrics that she appeared to believe in so heartfully.

Eight
Phone Call to a New Friend

September 9, 2017

Tell anyone whom I had ever loved, wrote Jacquelin.

Working through the list of people to call, I reached for Jacquelin's cellphone. Over-tired and reeling from shock, I summoned up the energy to begin the onerous task of calling her friends. There was a part of me that didn't mind the task because I wanted to keep talking about my sister. I yearned for insight into her final moments. I ached to understand her decision to end her life. The finality of her choice was incomprehensible, and I had to keep reminding myself to take deep even breaths.

When Jacquelin's cellphone lit up, her face stared back at me and filled the screen. The evenness of my breath dissipated and I had to swallow before I could look again. Jacquelin, appearing to wear a really bad wig, filled up the screen on the phone. Her pale face was surrounded by too much dark-brown. In another second, her face showed up with platinum-blonde hair in a side-part. In the next second, straight-thick-black hair framed her pale skin. Had she been alive and asked for my advice, I would have cautioned her against any of the colours and cuts. They were all too harsh. In the picture she looked alive, but not well. The gothic look made her appear like she was already in the morgue. But in reality, she *was* already there and it went through my mind that someone had played a mean trick. I clutched the cellphone and each evolving facial image deepened my despair. My jaw tightened. The rapid-fire appearance of her sad face caused me to lose my breath. It took me a few minutes to realize

Jacquelin had been experimenting with colour and styles. She had superimposed a variety of hair-style options onto a picture of her own unhappy face. Her experiment spooked me out and just about gave me a heart attack. To recover, I placed the phone on the counter and sighed long and hard enough to regain composure. Bearing in mind the last line in Jacquelin's note, "Any friends I have had and loved, let them know: e.g. Julianne," I pressed "contacts" on her cellphone.

To the best of my knowledge, Julianne was Jacquelin's most recent friend. A new friend. So, it might be surprising I called her first, but I did because she was the only person named in my sister's suicide note.

***

The first time I'd heard about Julianne was in July, 2016. I turned into my dad's driveway around eight-thirty in the evening and Jacquelin stood at the door and waved her arm at me to stop.

"Bev, I'm leaving. You'll need to back out."

It was a problem with single driveways. I parked my car on the street and by the time I walked up the driveway, she was preparing her breathalyzer.

"Where you off to?" I asked.

"The dog park."

She blew into the contraption and I heard noises coming from the machine.

"Sunnybrook?"

She nodded.

I knew the park well. "Isn't it a little dark down there?"

"There's lights."

Just one, I thought, and it only shone dimly over the pot-holed lot. The off-leash area had no lights, a fact I kept to myself. I also didn't mention my immediate thought about two-legged predators.

"Have you seen the Facebook page? There's been coyote sightings down there."

"We're careful."

A clue, I thought. I loved clues. "Oh, you meeting someone down there?"

"Bev. I gotta go…"

"Okay. See you later. Have a good night."

Before she pulled out onto the road, she stopped at the end of driveway and called out to me. "Oh…Dad's almost out of toilet paper."

Toilet paper? Why don't you get the freaking toilet paper? You live here.

I remained sullenly quiet about the toilet paper but I was no less irritated by the overgrowth of shrubs hanging into the driveway. Then I noticed the lawn—with all of the rain, it was lush and requiring a mow. My thought returned: Jacquelin lives here, perhaps during the breaks from her job search, she could get out the lawnmower.

Swallowing my annoyances and attempting to restrain my heightening resentments, I made a mental note to call the fellow my mother used to hire to take care of the grounds.

Inside, my dad sat in his swivel chair near the living-room window. The chair was placed for street-viewing, but not perfectly aligned to see driveway happenings.

"Hey Dad."

"Howdy." The smile in his voice helped to alter my mood.

"How about I make us a pot of tea?"

"Good idea." Another smile.

The kitchen was full of dirty dishes, so I had to make room on the counter for the teapot.

I put the tray down on the large coffee table within his reach.

"Dad, what do you think about the placement of Jacquelin's wicker garbage container on top of the kitchen table?"

I found it unsightly. Mel did too. Both of us were having difficulty adjusting to how our father's house had changed since our mother's death and after Jacquelin moved in. Both of us liked it neat and tidy, which was how our mother kept it. In hindsight, Jacquelin likely struggled to get out from under two opinionated sisters.

"I don't want to pull the tiger's tail," he said.

"Ah, good thinking."

My father explained the container was on the table so her dog Siron couldn't get into the garbage.

"Dad, out in the driveway, Jacquelin said she was going down to the dog park."

"She does that most nights."

"On Thursdays after I drop Jack off for his chemo, I take the dogs down there for a run. The park is behind the hospital. It's quite isolated. It would be worse at night."

"She meets a woman down there," he said.

He relayed stories about how the woman's dog played well with Jacquelin's dog, Siron. He seemed to enjoy describing one of the dog's bad habits, which was snatching poo-bags from people's hands.

"Dad, that's gross."

In a more congenial conversation at a later time, Jacquelin had told me about her budding friendship. Julianne's workday ended around seven and Jacquelin would meet her around dusk. They shared the experience of having an unwell parent. Julianne was a non-drinker and attended church. I really wanted my sister to have a friend, and hearing about Julianne offered relief. In the same conversation, she talked about an argument with Melody.

That's not new, I thought. "What about?"

"She got mad because I had to get off the phone to meet my friend who was expecting me in the park. I told her that I didn't want Julianne waiting alone down there."

"Sounds fair."

I was thrilled Jacquelin didn't want to be late or disappoint her new friend, not something I'd always witnessed from my end of our relationship. The two women texted one another to ensure neither one of them would be alone in the dimly lit parking lot.

"I want to cultivate this friendship," said Jacquelin.

My heart lifted some more. I liked hearing she made a new friend, someone she respected and a person she wanted to watch out for. It gave me hope about her ongoing sobriety and a move away from the dark sad life she had been living. At the same time I heard the echo of my mother's concern for Jacquelin, that like each of her other daughters, she should acquire at least one friendship of a person from a "good family."

Continuing to talk about her argument with Mel, she said, "Mel just kept talking. And since I had to go, I hung up on her."

"Sounds like you did your best to tell her why you had to leave."

I embraced her stand with Mel as a hopeful sign. I could even hear that she was concerned about hanging up on Mel. A few months ago, that kind of care wouldn't have been the case. I thought about miracles embedded in friendship. Yes, two women friends determined to get to the park on time so no one had to be alone in the dark. Empathy. Jacquelin's story gave me a glimmer of my sister at her best.

In my journal I wrote: *I'm getting my sister back.*

***

I called Julianne's number from my sister's phone which meant Jacquelin's name would light up on a person's phone screen. Julianne answered on the first ring.

"Hey you!..." I heard relief and imagined a big smile in Julianne's voice. "I was about to send out a search party—"

I held tight onto the cell and swallowed, "Is this Julianne?"

I noticed a nanosecond of silence and a breath. "Yes."

For extra support I leaned against our kitchen island with Jack on the other side.

"This is Bev, Jacquelin's sister..."

Sister, sister let me be your servant….Jacquelin, let me be your servant…

I told her why I was calling. I paused among breathy sighs. Her sobs did not come until many moments into the call. When she did cry, tears streamed down my own cheeks.

I will weep when you are weeping…

I told her I would have called her anyway, but that Jacquelin left a note, and that she was the only person named.

It was painful to hang up. I felt responsible for spreading so much grief. And because Julianne was with Jacquelin so close to the time she took her life, I secretly hoped for a clue or glimmer of meaning. A huge piece of me did not want to let Julianne go, yet there wasn't much more to say. Half way through the call I had a hunch it wouldn't be the last time we would speak.

In my journal, I wrote: *Jacquelin, the task you left me with is onerous. You also left me without any more chances for me to help you find an alternate path…Dear little sister, how can my heart not ache?*

***

After finishing my teary and emotional conversation with Julianne, Jack suggested I take a break. I couldn't, I told him. I was in task mode. I wanted to barrel through. I needed to do the hard stuff first, I said. I didn't know what else to do with myself except to take one pragmatic step at a time. I didn't want to stop connecting with the people who I thought would want to know.

Any friends I had and loved, let them know.

I took many deep breaths before I went to the contact list in her phone and I pressed the number for the next call. The phone rang just once.

"WHERE the hell have YOU been?" Loud exasperation spilled out with his words. Her phone log didn't show that she recently called him.

"Howie—" I spoke softly.

He didn't hear me.

Still loud and annoyed, I heard him say, "I've been calling and calling—"

"Howie…Howie…" I kept my voice low and slow. I was over tired and had to concentrate.

"Howie, it's not Jacquelin.…It's Bev…her sister."

For a second or two he went quiet. "W-where's Jacquelin?…Has something happened?"

"Yes, something has happened…Is someone there with you Are your parents there?" Jacquelin had spoken well of Howie's father. She had tolerated his mother.

From what Jacquelin said, I knew Howie as a vulnerable young man. I had a hunch he had little understanding of his own brokenness.

He became belligerent and impatient. "My parents are upstairs. What is it?"

I told him.

Did my words come out right? Was there a better way to have told him? I talked to Jack about this later and he said there was no good way.

There was a catch in Howie's voice. "HEY…hey…this is NOT funny…It's not right to do this kind of a joke—"

"No, no…this is not a joke. I wouldn't—"

Jack scowled from the other side of the kitchen island. He stepped closer. "If he's not going to listen, hang up."

I shook my head. I knew I could hold my own and I knew I could stay steady.

"Howie…Jacquelin took her own life…"

Tell people whom I had ever loved.

"Noooo…. No, no…." Over and over again he moaned. "Oh my God…"

I empathized with his shock. His voice filled with anguish. She wrote, *Don't suffer for me…*

I listened to him about how smart and courageous she had been and how much he loved her. Then he told me details hard to take in. She had been staying with him off, and on at his family's house. One time he found her in his father's workshop. With a wire around her neck.

I closed my eyes. "No, no, no…" I took a huge breath and let it out real slow. When I looked at Jack, his eyes had grown wider. I put up my hand to tell him I was okay.

In horror, I listened past Howie's regret. My chaotic mind reached for simplicity. I wanted my brain to help me make sense. Oh my God, I thought, Howie, I wish you had told me…He had tried to contact me at another scary time, like when he got to her house and witnessed a large man tossing her across the room. He asked for my help using Messenger, a platform I did not use. Months later, I came across the message.

"I just screamed and yelled at her." He gulped for air. "I told her she was stupid…And then I just started talking about myself."

So much regret. So much suffering.

Jacquelin had come across his formal diagnosis in a medical report. "Narcissist."

I leaned my elbows onto the island in our kitchen. I needed help holding up my head. I heard Jack clear his throat but I forced myself not to look at him. I knew he wanted me to hang up.

Howie kept talking. "I didn't tell anybody. I should have."

I stayed quiet but my mind was busy: yes, you should have told someone.

I remembered the long thin mark across Jacquelin's neck. I saw it months earlier and assumed it resulted from a botched neck tuck. Without a word to her, I had blamed the surgeon who had already altered her perfect nose. I thought the scar was a cosmetic surgery screwup.

Jack moved closer. "Sweetie…are you okay?"

I nodded.

"Howie, I'm saying goodbye now. Go and tell your parents what's happened. You shouldn't be alone. Please—"

He promised.

I was on the phone longer than was good for me. I could tell Jack thought the same. His unhappy eyes were on me.

Please Jack, let me do this my way, I thought. *I needed to do it my way.*

"The two of them had a 'pact.' They planned on killing themselves together. Now Howie thinks Jacquelin is the brave one."

I poured a glass of red wine and took myself to the couch. I sensed Jack's worried gaze.

"I begged him to talk to his father."

"I heard." Jack shook his head. "It's a mess."

"Yes, it is…He kept telling me he loved her and how fucking amazing she was…He said she's the strongest and smartest woman he's ever known."

I couldn't stop telling Jack about the conversation.

Jack ordered food.

I remembered Jacquelin talking about her affection toward Howie. He made her laugh. He didn't drink, and I said being with a non-drinker was good too. Her stories pointed to a relationship laden with complication, pain, hurt, and distrust.

Howie had confided in me months earlier. "If Jacquelin was well, she wouldn't have looked at me twice."

I didn't disagree.

When I had written about Howie in my journal, I referred to him as "Boy Toy," or "maybe-boyfriend" or "sometimes-boyfriend" or "on-and-off-boyfriend." I was angry for some of the ways he had treated her in the past. Not saying his name was the most I could do to hurt him back. When in his company, of course I called him by his name. In an email, he told me he preferred to be known as Howard. Jacquelin only ever called him Howie.

***

I met Howie the first time a few hours after picking up Jacquelin from court and becoming my sister's surety. I was surprised to see him at my front door because Jacquelin had neglected to tell me she had invited him over. I made lunch and he sat at our dining table.

"You have a very lovely home," he said.

After I served lunch Jacquelin told me that they would sit on the front porch.

"That's fine. You're not going anywhere…Right?"

"Right."

Within seconds, she was climbing into the back seat of his vehicle. I panicked.

Her behaviour was beyond my understanding. Was she not scared enough? Did she let Howie talk her into ignoring the rules? Did she think it was okay to lie to me?

Instead of calling the police, like I had been instructed to do if she wasn't complying, I called her lawyer. He was incensed and left me with no doubt I was within my rights to have her thrown back into jail.

When Howie dropped her off in the front of our house, an hour later, I exhaled with relief.

"Hi." Her voice was small and more high-pitched than normal.

"Hi?…I'm responsible for you. I signed an agreement—"

"I sat in the back seat."

"It's not just about not being in the front seat of a car." I reminded her of the rules. I told her what the lawyer said.

"He told me to read you the riot act, Jacq."

A big part of me blamed Howie. I had suspected he pressured her to go for that drive. She was vulnerable and unpredictable, which made it difficult to know how to find my way to helping her. In general, I felt nervously helpless, fearfully disappointed, and badly abused.

Months later, Howie called me. "Come and get your loser sister."

Okay, I thought, the guy is more trouble than I thought.

A couple of days before his call to tell me come and pick her up, I wrote:

Something isn't quite right. I'm not getting deep sleep. I'm hungry, even though my stomach feels full. I'm concerned about my sister's well-being. She is lost – still. [Journal entry: October 25, 2015]

"Okay. Should I come to your house?"

He couldn't have been clearer. "No. I don't want you anywhere near my parents' house."

"Where then?"

"Port Credit. Behind the Second Cup."

I used to sail out of the marina at Port Credit so I knew where I was going.

"When?"

"Two o'clock." He sounded like he was really pissed off. My stomach closed down.

Asking Jack to come with me was out of the question. His last chemo left him sick and since I had convinced him to take a "rescue pill" he slept. Before heading out I found the number for Women's Own, the only detox for women in the City of Toronto. I was given a central number to call. The dispatcher said a bed would be held until four o'clock, which didn't leave me much time to travel back and forth across the city.

I'd forgotten to ask Howie what kind of car he drove, and it wasn't until I arrived at the vehicle-packed lot that I panicked. I called his cell and left a message.

"I'm standing in the parking lot in front of the Second Cup."

I needed to use the washroom and the idea of not staying put in the lot made me nervous. I felt unsure what he would he do if he didn't find me. With apprehension I scanned the lot before slipping into the coffee shop.

I considered it bad luck to find the sign on the washroom door. "Under construction. Sorry for the inconvenience."

Frantic, I ran across The Queensway—a very wide roadway—to the No Frills. Like in most of those grocery stores, the washroom was in the far back corner. I checked my phone. No messages. When I got back behind the Second Cup I looked eagerly into the maze of cars. They weren't there, yet.

Knowing expressways leading into the City of Toronto begin to clog around three in the afternoon, and traffic crawls by four— never mind the downtown's gridlock—I was skating on the sharp edge of time.

Howie said to meet him at two-o'clock. My watch said three-thirty. The dispatcher at Women's Own said four. I cussed his tardiness and lack of attention to my calls. I was also pissed off at the inflexibility of the mental health system. The timeline was too strict and I heard no room for negotiation. And compassion? Not a hint of it.

Then I saw her. Waif-like and wavering in the wind, she stood against the backdrop of Lake Ontario. A bag sat on the ground beside her and Bella, her faithful Portuguese waterdog of the time, was on the other side. Both of them looked bedraggled, forlorn, and broken. My stomach throbbed.

I started up the engine. "Thank you, God."

There was no sign of Howie, and I swallowed my disgust.

"Jacquelin—" Her face turned, and I could tell she recognized me. It was hard to know what she was thinking. What I wanted most was for her to trust me. "Let's get you and Bella into the car."

I guided Bella onto the back seat and waited until Jacquelin sat in the passenger seat. I closed the door because I didn't think she was strong enough to do it herself. She did not look capable of running, but I had the need to hover because I didn't want surprises.

"Seat belt," I whispered.

Her hands shook.

"You're going to be okay." I whispered the words for her sanity as much as for my own. "We're going to get you some help."

I had enough power on my cellphone to call Women's Own.

"Jacquelin and I are leaving Port Credit now. I'm sorry we're going to be a few minutes late. I'm hoping you can still save the bed—"

The woman's apathy worried me. My sister needed compassion. Not indifference.

I drove north on Hurontario Road toward the Highway 401 East exit. Just before the ramp, a firetruck came out of nowhere, blasted its horn, and put on its siren. The sharp sounds played havoc with my nerves, and I almost jumped out of my seat.

"It's on your left," said Jacquelin. She sounded calm. "You need to get over." In that moment, she sounded more sober than I felt.

"I'm trying." In hindsight, I should not have been driving.

I thought about the boyfriend who wasn't there— the one who couldn't wait.

"I was expecting to see Howie back there. I thought he would have stayed with you until I arrived. I'm kind of surprised he left you and Bella in the lot."

She didn't say anything.

He had discarded her like unwanted waste. Used her up, depleted her, and left her at the side of the road. I didn't know his side of the story. Had he waited, I would have asked him how long she had been in this shape and if she had taken anything other than alcohol. A reasonable person would have waited.

"He's not treating you well, Jacquelin."

I was being careful. She was in crisis. So unwell. She had a disease, and getting angry at it didn't help. I was afraid she might crack. It was easy to be gentle with her, something I usually tried to do. My mother did the same. Sometimes one of us wouldn't get it right. If you didn't get it right, Jacquelin would just walk away. Saying "too much" to

Jacquelin was a risk we didn't want to take. On reflection, I see how I felt trapped and I believe my mother did too.

The sign for the Women's Own detox was buried in their overgrown hedge, and because of that, I drove by the building twice. I was relieved to guide Jacquelin up the stairs to the archaic wooden door with an intercom. I glanced at my watch. It was five o'clock.

A petite woman wearing jeans and a sweatshirt greeted us. She looked to be in her late-twenties. She held a plate covered with cellophane—a roasted chicken leg, sliced carrots, mashed potatoes and corn, all foods Jacquelin liked.

"Which one of you is the client?"

Jacquelin said nothing. I introduced myself.

"This is Jacquelin. I'm her sister, the one who called."

Still holding the plate, the woman asked Jacquelin to remove her jacket.

"We'll put your purse in a locker."

Hesitating and appearing less waif-like than earlier, Jacquelin said, "Yeah…okay…I'll need my cigarettes."

"This is a non-smoking facility."

The woman passed Jacquelin the meal and I hoped it would be hot enough to warm my sister's insides.

"I'm not hungry."

In *My Year of Magical Thinking*, Joan Didion wrote about the notion of offering food to a distressed person. "Don't ask, just give."

In a few sparse words, the worker indicated my role was done. It crossed my mind Jacquelin might change her mind and tell the worker she was coming with me. Thank God, she didn't. It was her first time there and she might not have known her stay was voluntary. I had said nothing about choice. I hoped she would stay. I breathed deep.

"Bye Jacq. Take care of yourself. I love you."

"Bye."

Her eyes were icy. Sometimes when we parted ways in the past, I could hear love in her voice. She'd give a soft giggle too and I'd get a strong hug. When Jacquelin started to drink heavily, all of that disappeared. Those absent gestures were part of grieving my sister even before she was gone.

Women's Own was housed in an old brown-stone house in Toronto with gorgeous Gothic architecture. The building's interior was cold and unwelcoming. Alongside the tiny vestibule was a cramped office; a window faced the square room, with four cots spaced six feet apart. No side tables or reading lamps. No posters espousing inspirational messages. No scents of nutritious food. One door led to the washroom, another opened to a yard or a lane. The glum physical space held no sense of hope.

Jacquelin was the only client. My curiosity was piqued: why the inflexible deadline? Were they expecting a rush of female substance abusers? Or an emergency? Aren't all detox situations an emergency?

As I walked down the stone stairs, I made a simple request: *please God, let the meal under the cellophane bring my broken sister some comfort.*

Inside the car, Bella hadn't moved and the greeting she gave was subdued. Was Bella depressed? Tired? Worried? What sense did she make of things? She knew something was up. Bella had known for a while.

"She's going to get some help, Bella."

I felt grit in her hairy curls, so when I got home I took her into the shower. *It was my first time showering with a dog.* Since company was coming—book club—I wanted Bella to look her best. Besides, dogs like Bella liked to be clean.

Eight years earlier I had driven to Niagara Falls with Jacquelin to meet the woman who bred Portuguese Waterdogs. When we arrived, no puppies were in sight. The breeder's only goal was to interview Jacquelin.

"Have you ever owned a dog before?"

Jacquelin described Zena, a German Shephard mix whom she got as a puppy and she talked about Yogi, adopted from the Humane Society.

"Portuguese Waterdogs are very different from Shepherds. Why do you want a portie?"

Jacquelin rhymed off her reasons—she had done her homework.

"Portuguese Waterdogs must be groomed on a regular basis," said the woman.

Jacquelin gave all the right answers and passed inspection. One week later we drove back to Niagara Falls to pick up her beautiful new puppy, Bella.

Bella became Jacquelin's soul mate. They went everywhere together. As my sister's life became more unpredictable, I noticed a worried Bella had started to retreat into corners.

At my house, about fifteen minutes before my book club's start, Jacquelin called.

"Come and get me."

Flabbergasted, I said, "No…you need to hang in…Get through it…The women will help you."

In my mind, rehabilitation at the renowned Homewood Health Centre in Guelph was the next step. My parents were on board with paying for Homewood.

The notion of paying for Jacquelin's rehab was out of sync with how our parents raised us. With earnings from our part-time jobs and summer employment us three girls paid the tuition for our postsecondary education. My parents covered the cost of our books and, as long as we lived at home, we were never asked to pay board.

But whenever there was an international school trip, like in my case, to Russia, it was on our dime.

After one of the times Jacquelin stayed at my parents' house, my mother told me she'd never seen anyone drink like that.

"Mom, it's hard...Especially for a mother..." I didn't say, "and an older sister who is sometimes the stand-in."

When it came to helping Jacquelin get sober, everyone in the family said, "Whatever it takes."

On the phone from Woman's Own, Jacquelin listed her complaints: under supervision, they reluctantly let her smoke at the back door. I heard negotiation in her voice. Jacquelin told them she suffered from migraines and needed medication.

"Jacq, they're not allowed to give you anything."

"That's bullshit. Anyway, they sent me to Toronto Western Hospital. They gave me valium."

The relief I had felt in response to getting her to Women's Own on time, disintegrated. So had the notion of holding a book club meeting free from inner turmoil. And then there was Jacquelin's familiar pattern: when she's not suffering as much— because she had secured valium —she shifts away from the idea of ways to stay well. Had she already forgotten about her horrible life? Did she forget being left at the curb like a bag of trash?

"You have to come and get me," she repeated.

"No, I don't. Stay there. Hang in. Tomorrow's another day—"

"Click." She hung up the phone.

Days earlier Jack had pointed out that I had started to talk to myself. And that evening was no exception, when I told myself, "It's real easy not to get it right. Bloody-hell—"

Knock, knock—

Three dogs, Winnie, Zachary and Bella, barked and yodeled to tell me the women had arrived.

I was pleased to pour wine.

"You have three dogs now?"

"Bella is a visitor."

"She's lovely."

"Yes, she is."

During the book club discussion, I remained quiet about the details behind Bella's visit. After my book-reading friends left, I realigned the pillows and topped up the dishwasher with glasses and small plates. Then I called my parents to tell them Jacquelin's whereabouts.

"She's here," interrupted my mother.

"Really?" Dumbfounded, I asked, "How did she get there?"

I overheard my mother repeat my question. "Jacquelin, how did you get here?"

"TTC." A surprise answer. Jacquelin had contempt for public transit.

"TTC," echoed my mother in her driest tone.

Her casualness annoyed me. In all fairness, my mother knew nothing of the day's drama. I wanted her to think between the blanks. What else could she say? What the hell was I expecting of her? Like me, there was nothing more to be done.

***

So, I went to an Al-Anon meeting. (The acronym Al-Anon derives from the combination of the first syllables in the words Alcoholics Anonymous.) In spite of knowing a friend's participation in Al-Anon brought clarity to her life, I cried as I walked through the door. Crying was allowed. I got involved in Al-Anon and stayed for over a year. The honest sharing of the men and women guided me through beginning episodes in my sister's drinking and the program taught me many lessons. On one of the evenings when I arrived early to help with chairs and refreshments, I was left with extra time to explore St. Clement's Anglican Church. Down the long hallway, the oak doors of the sanctuary were wide open, and that familiar oaky smell that I liked so much, invited me in. The only light in the sanctuary came through one of the stained-glass windows close to the altar. I knew the custodian was somewhere in the building and I considered if he found me there, that he might ask me to move on. I hoped not. I sat in a pew near the back and I stayed there until three minutes before the Al-Anon meeting started. I sat in the comfort of spaciousness that held the same woody smell of the church of my childhood and I savoured the silence and let myself be. What I came to know was this: how I walked with my sister in her brokenness, brought me to lean into my faith in a way I hadn't done before.

I have never forgotten when ML, a member of Al-Anon, told us how she responded to her son's call from a phone booth. He wanted to come home. Her voice cracked.

"No. Go away. Do not come back until after you get sober."

I imagined ML's suffering after she hung up the phone. She said self-doubt and second-guessing herself was eating her alive. To recover, she described drawing on her Al-Anon community and how she never stopped praying. If I had absorbed her message in time to share it with my mother, would either of us have followed her hard example? My parents and I had our moments of trying. Some would say that Jack practiced "tough love" best, but he told me later that he faltered too when he didn't tell Jacquelin exactly what was on his mind.

"What was holding you back?" I asked him.

"You."

"Me?"

"I didn't want to upset you."

Collective wisdom from professional recovery workers suggests family members don't always make the best helpers. They are too close.

***

On the evening of my book club, I said, "Mom, we're back at ground zero." I was angry. If I could relive the moment, I'd add, "And it is not your fault or mine." Homewood or any other rehab was off the table because Jacquelin had to be dry for at least seventy-two hours. They were following ML's example.

***

When I told Jack that Jacquelin had arrived at my parents, he repeated a line from before. "She's too much for them. There are too many soft landings."

I felt angry with him. I didn't feel up to his repeats.

Jack was never far away when I needed to talk about Jacquelin. Even through his cancer treatment, he'd listen. I did my best to check his energy, and on the days when he was really sick, I trusted myself to do whatever I could. I didn't call on help from other people and I wonder, even now, why I didn't reach out more. I was reserved to talk about Jacquelin's drinking problem with a few trustworthy friends. I wanted to protect her from judgement.

When it came to coping with Jack's cancer, which was really scaring me, I picked up a Wellspring brochure while browsing the resource centre at the Odette Cancer Centre. One time I attended a relaxing doll-making session. Another time I participated in a visualization. I was hoping to participate in a cooking session but I was only permitted to attend if Jack went too. In Jack's words, he had no interest in "eating nuts and berries" and "absolutely no intention of giving up red meat."

At a later time, two oncologists agreed and said to eat whatever he wanted to, including chicken wings. The radiation-oncologist who was convinced he only had months to live, said, "Eat all the steak you want."

At the Wellspring cancer support centre I did meet with a woman volunteer who was also a cancer survivor. She was lovely and we had a "nice little" chat. But what I wanted was to engage with another caretaker. To assist with that I turned to the internet and learned that I was supposed to be asking more people for help.

***

Garry was the last person listed in Jacquelin's cell phone log. Years ago, she had confided in me about him, a conversation I never forgot. Garry had a past history of swinging and after Jacquelin met him, the woman from the couple he swung with, resurfaced. When my sister shared this with me, I was protectively repulsed. According to Jacquelin, she told Garry to make a choice.

"Good call." I was hoping she'd give him a wide berth no matter what his decision. I didn't want my sister to just walk away, I wanted her to run.

To support my position, I told her the story about one of my professors. I was in second year and Peter and I had been married a few months. By coincidence we met the professor and his wife on the university's cross-country ski trails and ended up in an après ski conversation. When we mentioned our upcoming trip to Florida at the school break, we received an invitation to sail with them on their boat anchored there.

"Peter was thrilled and I was unsure."

"Why were you unsure?" asked Jacquelin.

"I had a bad feeling. That professor gave me too much attention. In his office in small-group meetings, he'd make comments about what I was wearing, even my hiking boots. An older and wiser woman in my group confirmed the ick factor. 'Just watch, he's going to ask you out,' she said."

"Did he?" asked Jacquelin.

"Yep. He invited me to an opera."

"Just you and him?"

"Yes, and I said 'no, thank you.' Then about half way through the semester, he called our apartment."

Seldom did we get an early morning call, so I remember jumping out of bed and sprinting for the phone. When I heard his voice, I did my best to sound awake.

"He said he was attracted to me...I froze trying to think of what to say...he said his wife and he had an open marriage. He kept a small apartment downtown."

"I guess you didn't expect that from one of your professors," said Jacquelin.

I chuckled. "Maybe I should have...he taught a course on variant family forms...Anyway, I stammered through the call. As a teacher, I liked him. But even if I wasn't married, I never would have been interested in a man at least forty-years older than me. I was so young and naive—I found the whole thing yucky."

"Hmmm."

"How did you feel when Garry told you?"

She paused to sip her coffee. "Weird."

I sensed it was more than that. She sounded sad. I think she liked the guy.

I didn't want to judge. "It's a lifestyle choice," I said. "One that isn't for everybody. One, I suspect, that has the potential for lots of heartbreak."

I could have, but didn't mention remembering the discomfort I felt about the unforgettable film, *The Ice Storm*, starring Sigourney Weaver and Kevin Kline.

"So, what happened with that professor?" she asked.

"He told me to find a new advisor for my independent project. That worked, because it meant I wouldn't be spending any more time alone with him in his office."

She sighed.

"It was still hard though, because I had two courses with him that semester."

She groaned. "Did he give you good marks?"

"Funny you should ask. No, the S.O.B. was harder on me than ever. I worked my ass off in that class and still got a skinny B."

I didn't process every detail of that long-ago memory just then, but the essence of Jacquelin's confusion loomed. I think her relationship with Garry was an on-and-off relationship. Maybe more of a friendship, or friends with benefits. She was pretty closed about it. All I knew was that they kept in touch. I suspected she reached out to him when she was in trouble. I was suspicious about his kind of help.

Despite the certainty of her death, it still felt like many pieces were missing. I had the yearning to understand what circumstances preceded her death. My phone call to Garry was grounded in desperation to hear something that would help me make sense of things.

Once again, I made the call from Jacquelin's phone. Garry was quick to answer. His voice sounded strong.

"Well, well, well...I was wondering when you were going to resurface. Where did you disappear to?"

"Garry?"

He expected to hear Jacquelin's voice. After a pause, I heard a definite shift in tone, "Yes?"

"This is Bev, Jacquelin's sister—"

He took a breath. "Oh..."

"I've got very bad news..."

Garry did not show up for Jacquelin's funeral.

Nine
A Falling Out Between the Cracks

September 10, 2017

I pushed through my list of people whom Jacquelin once loved and phoned John, my beloved ex-brother-in-law.

"Hey Bev, you caught me on the thirteenth hole." He sounded happy to hear from me. "How are ya?"

"Not so good. I've got bad news…but maybe I should catch you later…"

"No, no…what's going on?"

I gave him the news.

"WHAT?…Oh no…Not another death? Oh my God…"

He told me there had been a recent death in his family. John was remarried and the daughter of Lynda, his second wife, had died at the hospice just a few days earlier.

My re-entry into his life was at a difficult time—for both of us. On Facebook I'd seen pictures of Lynda's now-deceased daughter and her two children, both under five.

"I'm sorry to be having to tell you my news at such a sad time—"

In every phone call I made, I entered a person's day with a horrible heaviness and left.

"No, no…it's okay," said John. "You've done the right thing. It's just that there's been so much loss."

"Yes…"

Each person responded in their own way—gulps, wordlessness, and breathy sighs followed by grief-ridden explanations of disbelief and varied expressions of deep sadness. As always, my brother-in-law was gracious.

He said, "This is so crazy...Here you are telling me about Jacquelin's death and I'm golfing with the same two guys who were in our wedding party. It's a reunion. I haven't seen them for years."

I told him I remembered both fellas with fondness. Their wedding was in 1992. I recalled harp music floating in the summer air. The weather had been perfect for their afternoon wedding at the historic McLean House nestled on the edge of a Toronto ravine. Dressed in a gorgeous white gown with lace, Jacquelin strolled across the grass with my dad to where her future husband waited beside the unitarian minister.

In the eight years they were married I got to know my brother-in-law well. John liked doing family stuff. Jack and I often met up with him and Jacquelin in dog parks and auctions on the weekends. We shared dinners and watched movies on their expansive television. Jack and I thought the world of the man Jacquelin married.

***

After the call, Jack and I reminisced about their excitement about buying their first home. We had helped them with the move. I told Jack that one of Jacquelin's money-saving sacrifices was to park her car in an unkempt-gravel lot. It was a thirty-five minute walk away from her workplace behind the Eaton Centre. One time, I met her downtown for dinner and at the end of the night got a lift home. She and I walked along a seedy part of Dundas Street to get her car. When we got there a man was sleeping in the back seat of her Pontiac.

She banged on the window. "Hey you! Out!"

We stepped aside to let him stumble past us while grumbling a stream of profanities.

"Jacquelin, maybe you should lock your car."

"It's better not to. They'll just smash your window."

The poorly lit lot had no nighttime attendant.

"Jacq, it's a rough area to be walking alone in the dark."

"I'm not usually this late. Anyway, it's what I can afford."

In the throes of living out her strategies to pay off their mortgage, her then mother-in-law asked her son for a loan. When he relayed his mother's request, Jacquelin vehemently opposed the notion of paying off his mother's debt. Unfortunately, not long after, Jacquelin came across a letter from the bank. Upset and feeling betrayed, she called me.

"He went behind my back." Her disappointment was loud and clear.

From what I could tell, John's duplicity left no room for discussion. Appeasement was not coming anytime soon. Perhaps never.

"He was wrong to have done that Jacq. Plus, his mother was out of line to put him in that awful position in the first place."

I felt angry at his mother. She would have known they were working hard to pay off the house. To Jacquelin, I pointed out that every family has a culture of their own and I attempted to point out her husband's dilemma.

"I don't care. He was dishonest."

She was pissed off and beyond listening to how I saw things.

"You're absolutely right. He didn't tell you the truth and, yes, he went behind your back." Giving it another hook, I encouraged her to put herself in her partner's position. "What if Mom or Dad asked for money?"

She was hot. "They'd never do that."

True, they wouldn't.

In subsequent conversations, I pleaded with her. "Jacq, I'm sure John regrets—"

"I can't trust him."

Jacquelin told my parents about the attempt to borrow funds to cover his mother's debt. I suspect my father silently empathized with his son-in-law being caught between two women he loved. Not my mother—she was incensed. From her lens, Jacquelin's husband had done wrong and Jacquelin was right. There was no grey.

She told my mom what I had said. My mother was not pleased with me and I was left defending myself with her too.

"Mom, it's not just about disloyalty. I'm more concerned about Jacquelin. Her behaviour is terrible and I don't want to be around it."

I tried not to make it about me, but seeing my sister blinded by anger disturbed me. I was hoping my mother would help Jacquelin see past her rage.

"Mom, there are so many ways to respond to a problem like this. Meanness is not one of them."

Neither my mother or Jacquelin left space for forgiveness or reconciliation and I said too much. "Mom, I love her deeply. You know that. But I don't like what I'm seeing in her."

My mother must have heard enough from me because she hung up in my ear. She did a good job, once again, at shutting me down.

It was not just Jacquelin's conduct that I disliked, I wasn't nuts about my mother's either.

In the months that followed, my brother-in-law's misstep, I took another stab at talking to my mother about seeing all sides—Jacquelin's, John's and even his mother's. "Mom, he attempted to rescue his mother…it was a no-win for him. He made a grave error. But don't you think Jacquelin needs to cut him some slack? We all make mistakes. Where is forgiveness?"

My mother shut me down. "Don't be so naïve, Beverley."

Jacquelin maintained her resentment, and when she spoke to him, I overheard snips and snaps in her language. There were times when she did the same with me—snips and snaps that drilled into my core. My sister's acerbic tone bothered me, but her lack of empathy worried me more.

I stayed quiet until I didn't.

"Jacq, how you're treating your husband is hard for me to watch."

She accused me of taking his side. "You're my sister. You're supposed to be on my side."

"Jacquelin, we don't have to agree on this."

How did she hear me? Judged? Likely. Abandoned? Maybe. At the time it seemed that she wasn't listening, but perhaps she couldn't.

Months passed and closer to the dissolution of their eight-year marriage, Jack and I were chatting with John on the cottage dock when Jacquelin showed up smelling of perfume. (No one wears perfume at the cottage).

Without addressing anyone in particular, she said, "I'm meeting a friend in Wasaga. Don't know when I'll be back."

Without raising his head, John muttered under his breath. He stared at the ground and looked defeated. While Jack turned away, I watched my sister walk up the rugged-stone steps in her high-heeled sandals.

"I think this is the last time I'll be at the cottage," he said.

I rubbed his back. "What Jacquelin is doing and how she is treating you, isn't right."

"She needs to sow her wild oats," said John, "She's never really had a chance to do that…I'll just have to wait and see."

Their marriage ended soon after that weekend. She bought him out, and he purchased a house closer to where he worked. At the time they had two dogs and two cats. She told him to take the pets, which he did willingly.

I said to Jack, "It's bad enough splitting with your spouse, but I don't understand how she can give up Yogi and Zena and the cats."

After our falling out, things weren't really the same between Jacquelin and me, something that became apparent at Easter. No one in the family had organized a dinner or brunch, so I called my mother on the phone.

"Mom, I know this is really last minute, but Jack and I would like to have everyone over for Easter dinner tonight."

After an intake of breath, my mother said, "Jacquelin has invited us over for brunch."

"Everyone?"

"Y-yes, I think Melody and Owen are going—"

There was an awkward pause.

"O-okay then," I said.

Hearing the telephone conversation come to its end, Jack asked, "What's up?"

"Everyone's going over to Jacquelin's for brunch."

"Great, let's go—"

"No, you don't understand. We're not invited."

Looking at me, "You're kidding."

"No, I—I'm not." I felt shaken, Easter is a big deal for me and so were family gatherings.

"This is bullshit." Jack was angry and I was sad.

"I'm going for a walk."

"Want me to come with you?" Walking was not really his thing.

"No, that's okay…I'm going to Mount Pleasant."

Mount Pleasant cemetery, with its trees and wildlife, was my "go to" place.

"Okay…Sweetie…We'll do something when you get back."

When I arrived home from my walk, Jack told me that he called my father.

I winced. "What did you say?"

"I told him what I thought."

I groaned at the prospect of conflict between my husband and my father. "Jack?"

"I told him it's not right. It's hurtful. I reminded him that he has *three* daughters."

"What did he say?"

"He asked me what I expected him to do, and I told him."

I hadn't thought about it at the time, but my dad was in the same position as Jacquelin's ex-husband—caught between the people he cared about.

I took in a breath. Everything felt messier than it had to be.

Still seething, Jack said, "I told him that he needs to talk to his daughter. I told him what's going on isn't right. Then I hung up."

Other than in my conversation with Jack, no one in my family ever mentioned the phone call again.

My sister's marriage was over, and, my relationship with her was badly bent.

John remarried, and by all accounts, he found his soul mate.

***

After interrupting his golf game to tell him about his ex-wife's death I felt responsible for leaving him with such devasting news so I slipped into care-taking mode and called Lynda, John's wife.

When she answered, I said "I'm Jacquelin's sister…I'm sorry to tell you this but I just caught your husband on the golf course and I gave him very bad news—"

"Yes—" Her voice was soft and gentle.

"I'm calling to let you know I laid a real heavy on him—"

"Yes, Bev, I—"

"I had to tell him that my sister died and I know it was really bad timing…Oh, my God…I am so, so sorry about your daughter, Jennifer…such a tragedy…such a loss—"

"Bev…Bev, he already called me…He's okay." After exchanging comforting words about her loss and mine, she asked, "When is the funeral?"

Ten
A Blessing

September 11, 2017

Reverend Ian had agreed to bless Jacquelin's body after it was released by the coroner. We met at the funeral home. Jack would have come but he was recovering from his chemo treatment.

When I arrived, Jacquelin's pine coffin was in the funeral home's small chapel. Ian was there too, in his robes, holding the Book of Common Prayer. To feel as close as I could to my deceased sister, I flattened the flesh of my palms against the coffin. It was smooth under my fingers but I still felt I couldn't get close enough. Ian prayed out loud, I mumbled along.

Give rest, oh Christ, to thy servants with thy Saints, where sorrow and pain are no more, neither sighing, but life everlasting…

He chanted the twenty-third psalm. I sang too.

The Lord is my shepherd; therefore can I lack nothing. He shall feed me in the green pasture, and lead me forth beside the waters of comfort.

Comforted by the words, I wondered if the psalm had ever reassured her. I pictured Jacquelin and I together in the ravine. I envisioned us swimming around the island at the family cottage.

After the blessing, Ian suggested we talk. I asked the tall hovering woman who worked at the funeral home if there was place where we could chat and when I asked, I sensed her hesitation.

We followed her into the foyer where she pointed to a door. "You can use this room."

She stood at the threshold as Ian and I settled on the chairs. Like Joyce and I had noticed one day earlier, the woman's sullen demeanor seemed no less strange. When she closed the door and left us in private, I breathed with more ease.

"Ian, I can't thank you enough for your prayers and blessing my—"

"You are very welcome, Sister." His voice was as warm as his brown eyes. "Now tell me about Jacquelin. What was she like?"

I took a deep breath from the rawest place in my heart and shared details easy to talk about.

"She was someone who liked scented candles, hot baths, and music."

I told Ian about the times when she and I sat on the carpet with my guitar and a pile of sheet music.

"We sang a lot of Simon and Garfunkel. 'Bridge Over Troubled Waters' was a favourite."

When you're down and out…When evening falls so hard …I will comfort you…

I remembered us singing Carole King's "You've Got a Friend," and Yip Harburg and Harold Arden's, "Somewhere Over the Rainbow," like we really meant it.

Where troubles melt like lemon drops
Away above the chimney stops
That's where you'll find me…

After her death, the tension between comfort and discomfort in the lyrics jumped out at me in ways I had not noticed before, and I wondered if either of us had felt the dark disquiet. Seems those songs drew both of us in.

Ian kept listening while I kept talking.

"Jacquelin loved sushi."

I didn't say anything about the discomfort that played out on the day in Waterloo. Jacquelin's new job was there. She needed to find a place to live, so we went looking for an apartment. I drove. After an unproductive morning, we broke for lunch. She suggested sushi.

"I don't eat raw fish," I said.

But she didn't listen and ordered far more than either of us could eat. At the time, I thought her self-indulgent and unkind. This was before I had a clearer sense that she was in some kind of trouble.

Continuing to share my thoughts with Ian, I said, "She loved to dance."

I described how we'd push away cottage couches so the women in our family could dance. The men talked and looked on from chairs around my grandmother's dining table.

"In the summertime, on weekends, my sister and I used to run on the cottage road."

I remembered she loved yogurt, dogs, strong coffee, and flowers—especially roses. Yellow was her favourite. She loved a baked potato, tangerines and bananas. I gave Ian all of these details.

Through the door's little window, I caught sight of the buxom woman in the funeral home's foyer. I thought she wanted to go home, but Ian, who was in full-pastoral-care mode, was unrushed and asked me another question.

"What about your other sister?"

"Melody? She was born in 1960. A Taurus like me…so was my mom."

He smiled but didn't pursue it.

***

I didn't talk to him about my vivid memory of the morning my mother went into labour. I'd been woken by unusual sounds so I wandered into the living room to find my mother lying on the couch. My dad was holding her hand. Assured everything was okay, I went back to bed. A few hours later on his way to the hospital, my dad dropped me at my paternal grandmother's house. My grandmother took me to school and when she brought me back at lunchtime, my dad was waiting in her kitchen.

"You have a baby sister." His voice was filled with delight.

I was happy too. But within days I'd grown tired of having a baby in our house. Perhaps I longed for the previous "single-child" status-quo.

"Take her back to the hospital," I said.

My parents entered into a charade: Melody was carefully tucked into the white portable bed with chrome handles. They put on their coats, and, as my father reached for the door handle, he turned to look at me sitting in the middle of the couch.

"We'll be back soon."

I had a change of heart.

"She can stay," I said.

"Pardon?"

"I want her to stay."

What I told Ian was that from the get-go, Melody had a lot of energy. She was hardy, and I can still picture her at three-years of age ploughing through the bush barefooted. My mother, who had a deep-seated fear of snakes, was horrified.

"Melody…get out of there!"

Other than a few scrapes and scratches on her arms and legs, Mel came out unscathed. Our dear neighbour, Mrs. Peterson, one of the aunt-like people in our lives, tried her best to steer Melody clear of the blueberry patch she had hoped to harvest. To dissuade Melody from stomping on the berries, Mrs. Peterson promised fresh pie and blueberry loaf.

Our old eight-millimeter movies—later transferred onto video-cassette—confirmed Melody's distaste for her playpen whether it was the one at the house in Toronto or at the cottage. Judging from the image of her tear-streaked face and stubby little fingers clutching at the wooden railings, I imagined what she wanted us to understand.

"I want out! Get me out of here…Now!"

My parents came up with an idea of how to release my mother from worrying about their fearless toddler wandering into the woods or toward to the lake. When my dad got back from the hardware store, he was carrying a large bundle of metal fencing. Once trees were marked, my parents unwound the bundle of interlocking wire to reach around the large circle of pines on the back part of the property. A climb-proof gate was built, and Mel's toys—bike, carriage, sandbox, and eventually a swing set—were placed inside. Every summer my forceful little sister, at three, four, five, and six years old, was corralled for her own safety. And for my mother's sanity. In hindsight, for my sanity too.

The video showed me with our cousins visiting Melody's pen. It appeared that our blond and tan German Shepperd, Nipper, was her most frequent companion. Those early cottage days were sometimes lonely for Mel and, from what she told me later, she was often unhappy. Perhaps she thought of herself as a captive in the pines.

When Mel neared the age of five, she was considered a handful by most people who knew her. With the help of another couple, my parents hoped to get some extra cottage work done so they arranged for her to stay with my aunt and uncle and their five children. My then nine-year-old self and Nipper, because apparently neither of us presented any trouble, went to the cottage with my parents. It was assumed Mel and Laura, my aunt Audrey's youngest daughter, would play nicely together. When we picked Mel up at the end of the weekend, all of my cousins—Sharron and Laura and their three brothers stood on their front lawn in Willowdale. From the back window of Dad's station wagon, I watched my male cousins' dramatic jumps of joy while waving an enthusiastic goodbye to Mel.

"Goodbye Melo-monster! Goodbye."

Sharron and Laura were there too, but I don't recall their display of delight to see my sister go.

At a family reunion two years after Jacquelin's death, my cousin Sharron shared her fifty-year-old memory of the same story of how Mel came to be known as Melo-monster. She added more detail.

"You know how my brothers loved their television..."

"Oh dear..." What's coming, I wondered.

"Your sister just LOVED to remove the knobs from OUR television and THEN put them somewhere."

Sharron laughed heartily and employed dramatic pauses in her telling. "Yeah, your poor mother, what she must have had to endure."

"Hmmm..." I had a pretty good idea.

"And my brothers...they didn't like it one bit...And on top of it, at one point on that weekend, Melody couldn't remember where she put the knobs and of course that made everything far worse...It wasn't funny at the time...but now it's hysterical." She slapped both thighs when she laughed. Sharron enjoyed telling the story about the sleepover and television knobs and how she told it got me laughing too.

Knob stealing was featured in the family video I had made for my parents' Christmas present. One scene showed the television sitting kitty-corner in the living room. It had little bare spokes sticking out. No knobs. On Christmas day when my family watched the family videos, Mel's then-husband asked a pointed question.

"Hey...how come that television has no knobs?"

All eyes set on Melody and the story was shared again. I couldn't be sure if Jacquelin had heard it before but I noticed she unearthed a huffy sigh as she cast a knowing-glance in Mel's direction.

"Figures," she mumbled, with eyes rolling.

Did she take your things, too? I wondered.

In my own adolescence, television knobs didn't concern me. However personal things—like a hair brush, curling iron, or a blow dryer—did. Humour aside, I could fully identify with my adolescent cousins and their frustration and extreme sense of helplessness. When it came to my own stuff, which I needed in the mornings while attempting to get ready for school, I recall asking my mother if she thought Melody might be a kleptomaniac.

At the funeral home where the buxom woman paced outside the tiny room with the small window, Ian listened with intent.

"Bev, when you talk about the cottage, your face lights up."

"Yes...I love it there. My family had the best time together. And now it's my sanctuary."

I envisioned myself sitting at the end of the dock with my feet dangling in the water. The truth is, I didn't. The reason had to do with an experience when I was nine years old in 1964, the same weekend Mel was staying with our cousins at my aunt's and when she acquired the title "Melo-monster."

Gloria and Russel, a childless couple, were the friends helping out at the cottage, which at the time was still just a shell. After an early start to the workday, the adults went to the shore and they took me with them. A photograph confirms it isn't a swimming day. We are fishing and it is warm enough to wade. The picture captures me standing at the shoreline with one leg in water up to my knee. My other leg is on shore, firmly planted on the rock with short pants rolled up. I'm facing the sun and there's enough wind to gently blow my chin-length hair westward. Standing as still as a statue, I resemble a young Audrey Hepburn. Russel is sitting by the fire, singing and playing his guitar. I liked when he did that, so I am likely listening.

The photograph didn't capture what happened next. I must have felt a presence, because I glanced down. That's when I saw the head of a very large water snake, black and thick, it had wrapped itself around my skinny leg. Three loops. Here, I point to my mother's deep-seated fear of serpents, for by the time I was nine, I'd witnessed a number of her hysterical screaming fits. (Land clearing stirs up reptiles.) Fortunately, the snake around my leg wasn't touching my skin—yet.

Without a sound, I was quick to pull my leg up and out of the coil. With both feet firm on the ground, I released a scream from the depths of my throat that no doubt rivaled the volume of my mother's high-pitch-snake-screeches.

Mom was standing about five yards away, and while still screaming I bounded in her direction. Until, red-haired Gloria stepped into my path. I remember how she spoke to me—firm, succinct and direct.

Gloria raised her hand to the height of her shoulder.

"Stop screaming!"

And she swung the flat of her hand until it stopped in its swing and landed hard against my face.

Smack.

Stunned, I forgot about the long black snake and I stopped making noise. Russel did too. Singing and strumming ceased.

The five-minute experience of the snake wrapping itself around my leg, followed by the stinging slap on the left side of my face, continues to shape my behaviour. I love the lake. It brings me endless joy and serenity. I kayak, canoe and row across the lake's waters. And I swim in it. But never do I dangle my feet. I have tried to remember, but still I cannot conjure up what happened next on the shore. I'm pretty sure the story ended with my mother's arms wrapped around me. I wish someone had taken another picture.

Relaying stories to Ian about my sisters brought comfort. I remembered swimming together with Jacquelin around the island across from our cottage. When "something" slimly brushed a leg our squeamish cries and high-pitched squeals startled one another. Water snakes came to mind. Swimming through the weeds was always more possible when we did it together.

***

Before Jacquelin was born, the Watson girls—Heather, Laurie and Cindy—had a cottage two lots away. The three sisters were close in age, something I recognized as fortunate. If anyone had asked me for my advice about how far to space out pregnancies, I would have pointed to the family plan of Mr. and Mrs. Watson as an acceptable model.

Like Jacquelin came to do when she got older, the two youngest, Heather and Laurie, shared my interest in being in or on the water. They had a wooden fishing boat with a small motor and so did I, but my family's boat was of aluminum. We spent our youthful summers scouting trails on the crown land islands and traipsing into the forest for the perfect fort lot. Years later, my dad told me he knew where to retrieve the old tools I took from his shed.

"How'd you know where they were?" I asked him.

I remember his smile. "Do you think we don't know where you were?"

I didn't think so. At the cottage, I felt free from parental surveillance.

Heather and Laurie were tomboys. Perhaps I was described that way too, but not to the extent of their fearlessness about picking up frogs and other reptiles. Me? I liked such creatures very much, but from a distance. When they celebrated a bullfrog capture, I'd feel regret. I really didn't want the frog to be caught and, when the hunt along the shoreline came up empty, I silently celebrated. If the hunt was successful, that meant frogs were kept captive in cages under their cottage where Heather and Laurie thought their care of them—provision of food, water and visits—was adequate. I told these girls just about everything, but I was never honest enough to say I didn't think frogs should be kept captive. The one person I talked to about it was my dad.

"I don't think it's fair to the frog," I said.

"No, I don't either."

Knowing they were cramped in cans with a perforated-lid held down by a rock, bothered me. I remember my subtle hints to my much-loved friends.

"Are you sure they can breathe in there?" Yes. "Is there enough water?" Yes.

Thinking about those trapped critters reminds me of Heather-Violet who is a good neighbour's daughter. Among her 2015-travel-tales in China, was a story about releasing dogs trapped in back-room cages of a restaurant.

Riveted by her story, I said, "HV, you took a real chance."

"I know. But I didn't care."

Heather-Violet wanted those dogs to run free, and at age twenty-something she had the agency to make it happen. My twelve-year-old self never followed through on my idea of kicking off the lid so the captured bullfrogs could go free. Yet, my remorse about their captivity was immense.

It is important to say that close to the end of the summer, my cottage friends, sisters Heather and Laurie, tipped the cans, and the bull frogs went free.

When Mel turned six or seven, my parents dismantled her cage among the pines, and I was then charged with bringing middle-sister Mel along with me wherever I went.

"Why does she have to come with me?" I asked.

"Because she's your sister."

"Yeah...but..."

I suggested Mel could bring a friend from the city. Had Melody been "easier," it might have happened. Instead, she was left under my watch. My responsibility.

Mel's legs weren't as long as mine. Shorter legs were only a problem when I was in a tree house and heard my sister calling from the bottom of the tree.

"Can I come up?" she cried.

Teddy, the oldest Watson sibling, had strategically placed the ladder's first rung such that none of his sisters, while they were still short, could enter his treehouse. By the time his sisters and I were all capable of reaching the first rung of the tall climb—and Teddy had moved on—Mel was still too little.

"No, your legs can't reach. You better go home," I told her.

Unhappily, she did, and, not long afterwards, I heard my father's voice bellowing through the trees, "BEVERLEEEEY…"

Of course, I didn't want my little sister to be forever stuck in the cage among the pines. That would have been unjust. But at the time, her release stunted my freedom. At the time, it felt complicated. At the time, it felt unfair.

Polite and well-behaved, I was the daughter who watched and listened. I remember observing Jacquelin's silent watchfulness too. In that way, Jacquelin was like me—a quiet observer.

My face tingles as I write so I know something in this small realization matters. I hadn't thought about this shared characteristic between us at different temporal stations of our lives. I wonder if this subtle similarity shaped our relationship? Were we more alike than either of us knew? [Journal entry]

In hindsight, I think I wanted us to be more similar in nature than we were. I believe I wanted Jacquelin to be more like me—discerning and pragmatic—that way, I thought she'd stay out of trouble. If Jacquelin picked up on that, I wonder if she couldn't breathe.

***

Under the supportive asylum of his pastoral care, when Reverend Ian invited me to talk about my sisters and especially, Jacquelin, the stories he encouraged me to tell became the framework for the eulogy I wrote. Talking to Ian was my dress rehearsal to talk about my sister at her funeral.

Eleven
A Meeting of Weeping Strangers

September 11, 2017

On the hot sweaty night at the drop-in group, Alex told us about the eight-week program called Support for Survivors of Suicide. He explained how each survivor was matched with two trained volunteers, who were also survivors of suicide loss.

When I asked him to add my name to the list, Alex said he would call me when a space opened up. Eager to connect with others confronted by this tragedy, his phone call could not come soon enough.

Earlier in the same day, I called my friend Rick to tell him about Jacquelin's death. We had a tender conversation. He told me that one of his nephews, his sister's middle son, had died by suicide. I sensed Rick's sorrow about his sister's loss and a deep understanding of mine.

A few minutes after Rick and I said goodbye, he called back to say he had spoken about me to his sister, Betty-Lynn.

"She'd be more than happy to talk to you."

The next day Betty-Lynn called me from her home in Saskatchewan and we talked on the phone for a long time. By the end of the call, we were no longer strangers. Within days, she sent me the name of a therapist in Toronto. A little while later, when she came to visit Rick, she and I sat together in the shadowy back room of the Bean coffee shop on Queen Street in The Beach. We talked for hours, and at different intervals of our intimate conversation, tears streamed down one of our faces.

Friends' wisdom and resources kept showing up and when it did, I let other people's generosity into my life. I embraced support with an openness that was unlike how I perceived anyone in my family accepting help from others. I was living outside my family script. Perhaps it was because both of my parents were pragmatic and apt at resolving problems themselves. That is why seeking and receiving help from others was not modelled in my family. If either of my parents sought emotional help, they were discrete. From what I could tell, asking for support was considered a weakness. Perhaps that is why my career in the helping profession never got entirely revered by anyone in my family.

I had to unlearn what my parents had instilled in me about "going it alone." In my mid-thirties when I first sought help, I had to push away the notion of therapy as an indulgence. When I was on the cusp of quitting the sessions, my then-therapist described a study about men who are in therapy excelling in the workplace.

"Really?" Challenging her, I asked, "Do you have a therapist?"

"Not right now, but I was in therapy for years. I was in intense supervision. My supervisor died a couple of years ago." She described their relationship and I decided it was something I wanted.

Eventually I came to embrace therapy as a time and place to learn about one's self. My therapist coached me to embrace vulnerability as an opportunity, not a liability. Prior to working with her, vulnerability was considered a weakness in my family and that's why I had worked hard at hiding it. She helped me rethink it, work through it. I came to experience that a lot of good comes from unbridled vulnerability. To be vulnerable is to be human.

How I came to embrace vulnerability and accept the support and loving kindnesses offered to me were in stark contrast to Jacquelin's inability to reach out and take advantage of resources. Jacquelin, who was like my mother in so many ways, had a horrible time asking for help.

Twelve
Telling Dad Six Days Later

September 12, 2017

The all-purpose neat and tidy activity room was in the basement of the nursing home. To the right of the double doors was a long counter with a sink and cupboards. Another wall sported the residents' art work. Two tall Ikea shelves housed books, musical instruments and craft supplies. In a gallant attempt to detract from the view of car tires in the parking lot, a vibrant mural, designed by a local youth group, surrounded the window-well.

A table with chairs sat in the middle of the square brightly lit room. Jack positioned my dad's wheelchair close to the table, between Mel and me. (I felt bad that Mel's husband Owen, couldn't be there with her. He had been sick, so it wasn't okay for him to be in a nursing home.) Jack and Ian stood. We could all see each other's faces.

I spoke first. "Dad, we've got some very sad news."

"Did someone die?"

In our stunned silence my stomach sank and my eyes locked with Ian's. My first thought: is my dad psychic? Or was he assuming there had been a death because Reverend Ian was in his presence? At another time when I'd pointed out that an orthodox priest had entered the building, he had said, "Oh, someone must have died."

"Yes," I said. "Someone died."

"Violet?"

"No, not Violet." My dad's second oldest sister was ninety-nine.

"Who then?"

Watching him, I breathed deep.

"Jacquelin."

"JACQUELIN!" My father's words came out in squeal. I witnessed pure shock.

No one missed his despair. "JACQUELIN DIED?!"

My body shook. Mel's eyes filled with tears. Everyone's eyes misted over.

"Yes," I said. "Jacquelin."

He leaned forward in his chair. He stayed very, very still. Then he lifted his head to look at me. He asked the hard question.

"How did she die?"

It was the question that Mel and I knew he had to ask. We had agreed to tell him the truth. Some people had suggested if it were them, they wouldn't. Our father deserved the truth and besides, we didn't lie to one another about such matters.

I gulped. For extra strength I looked around the circle. Mel looked frightened. My eyes stopped at Ian. He nodded. Taking in air, I answered my dad's question.

"She took her own life."

My dad turned in my direction. "She committed suicide?" His enunciation of the word "suicide" struck me.

Inhaling, "Yes."

Tears streamed down distraught faces. He waited a few seconds until he asked me his next question.

"How?"

Back to Ian: our eyes locked. He nodded.

Releasing air, I said, "She hung herself."

My father gasped. His head dropped into his large strong hands. He moved his head from side to side.

"Why didn't she come and talk to me?" He leaned over his knees and sobbed.

Such a good question. His weak voice was strong enough for us to hear. Other than tears and misty eyes, love and wordless empathy filled the room. Ian's head lowered.

In the silence interrupted by sniffles, my dad repeated his question. "Why didn't she come and talk to me?"

I only had a hunch. Gathering the courage to speak, I said, "Dad, she's been unhappy for a long time—"

He sat up straight and shifted his back against the wheelchair.

No longer soft, he said, "The stupid, stupid girl..." As those words left his mouth, I watched him move his head moved back and forth, "No, no, no..."

We heard pain. We had it too. No one had stopped weeping.

Standing in the depths of my own sorrow, I watched everyone else's. The finality of Jacquelin's death hung in the air. The words I couldn't stop saying when I found her kept echoing through my mind. "Jacquelin, what have you done? Jacquelin, what have you done?"

My father had another question.

"Where?"

I didn't hesitate. I wanted to tell the truth. Gently I said, "At the house. In the den."

I didn't say I suspected the easily accessible tool box on the floor in the corner was likely part of her resourcefulness. My father never forgot where he put a tool. He knew her well enough and didn't ask.

No one had moved from the circle with Dad in the wheelchair, Mel on one side, and me on the other. Jack and Ian remained standing the whole time. Ian invited us to pray. We lowered our heads. I believe we were thirsty for words that might help sort out the pain. Ian prayed for my family's sorrow, grief, and despair. Each of our names were in his prayers. He asked God for help. He prayed for Jacquelin. Then he invited us to hold hands and join him in saying the Lord's prayer.

"Our Father, who art in heaven..."

There was a knock at the door. I glanced at my watch. "Agh..." It would have been the activation coordinator. I wanted my family to have more time.

"Hallowed be thy Name..."

I thought the director might have explained the situation to the activation coordinator. Perhaps they could have altered the schedule.

"...Give us our daily bread..."

But what I realized later about the well-oiled nursing home was that everything went by the clock.

"...Thy power and Glory.... forever and ever. Amen."

After the prayer, I opened the door. Residents in wheelchairs looked at me in anticipation. The interruption wasn't their fault.

Within minutes someone guided us through a maze of hallways into the abandoned lobby. Ian and Jack took the stairs. Jack said he wanted to get back to our house to check on the dogs. Ian said he'd speak to me later. With Mel at my side, I pushed the wheelchair into the elevator. No one spoke.

The nursing home was nestled between a six-storey condo and a fire station. In front was a large courtyard with raised gardens that lined a wide cement path to the front door. The tree branches formed an arch over the walkway. Days later, I saw a scurry of squirrels and a host of sparrows had found homes in those trees and the hedges. Life goes on, I thought.

Mel, being a smoker, handed my dad a cigarette and took one for herself. It wasn't long before two women residents, also smokers, joined us. They took seats on the wooden bench. Mel sat on the other bench and I stood.

When Donna and Julie introduced themselves, I could tell they had already befriended my dad.

Julie asked, "How are you today, Fred?"

He shook his head. "Oh...not so good."

"Why? What's happening?" asked Donna.

"My daughter died." *Yes. Our sister died.* He hadn't minced his words.

"Oh no..." said Donna.

"Oh dear...what happened?" asked Julie.

He spoke in a low voice. "She committed suicide."

"Oh Fred, that's terrible." Their compassion was palpable. I wondered about their stories. I sensed familiarity in their response to my father's distress.

"Yes. It is terrible." He held the butt between two fingers. His hands shook. He had smoked quickly. I came to know later that when he smoked quickly, he shook.

"Dad, want another?" asked Mel, lighting one for him before he responded.

"Yes, I will take another."

Mel finished her cigarette and put it in the ashtray. "If I leave now, I'll catch the train in time."

"Yes, dear…you should go," he said.

I didn't feel ready to leave. After the two women smokers went back into the building, I was alone with my dad.

"Dad, we'll want to have a nice funeral for Jacquelin, right?"

"Yes. Why don't we do the same as we did for your mother?"

"Sure. I thought that's what you'd want. Is it okay if I take care of things and keep you in the loop?" The question was rhetorical. I knew I was the person to take care of things. And I knew that he knew that too.

Slumped over, he nodded. "That would be best."

"Okay…Do you want to call your brother?"

"Yeah, let's do that. I need to tell Billy…"

Pulling out my cellphone, I connected with my uncle. After that difficult and forthright conversation, exhaustion overtook my father. Sadness too. Deep sorrow. It was hard for me not to weep.

"Dad, how about I take you upstairs, so you can lie down?"

"Yeah. I'd like to lie down."

I wheeled him into the building's elevator and then down the long hall to his room. Once in bed, he sighed deeply.

"It's been a hard day," I said.

"Yes, it sure has."

We talked a little bit longer before saying goodbye.

"Bye, bye dear. I love you."

"I love you too, Dad. I'll see you tomorrow."

I imagined his aloneness. I guessed how he was missing my mother. I wished he didn't have to be alone, at such a hard time, in the company of strangers.

At the door's threshold I looked back. His head sunk into the pillow and his eyes had not followed me to the door. They were closed. In the depth of another loss, he never asked why we had not told him sooner. I would have told him the truth about that too. At the door, pausing to watch him, still and contemplative, I understood his grief. He had tried to save her too. But at the same time, what sense could he possibly make of a daughter's choice? Even of his own choices to help her?

Later in the day, I felt compelled to talk to Howie's father. I needed to tell him about his son's suicide pact. Once I found his work number, I went outside because it was warm enough for me to make the call from our front porch.

"Suicide ideation is very common after a death by suicide," I said. "From what Howie said to me, I'm afraid he could be considering taking his own life."

I heard anguish across the line. After more talking, he said, "I'll call his therapist."

"Good idea," I said. "We don't want another loss."

Howie's father asked me about funeral plans.

"Will you be attending?" I asked.

"Of course. We all loved Jacquelin. We'll be there."

I knew I'd made an important call.

Any friends I had and loved, let them know…

Thirteen
Watching From the Street

April 2013

I scanned the book shelf for an engaging read and I thought Carol Shields's *Unless* was an excellent pick. I bought her award-winning novel when it was published in 2002, and remembered not wanting to put it down. I have never forgotten Reta's attempt to oversee her nineteen-year old daughter, Norah. In 2002 when I read the book for the first time, I was not watching over Jacquelin the way I was when she became unwell. How Reta tried to keep track of her daughter was different from my approach. Reta drove to where Norah sat on the sidewalk in front of Honest Ed's. She watched in the morning. I observed at night while sitting in my car under the dim shadow of a street light. I spied on my sister's house. I did that because I'd run out of ideas. Sitting alone, Norah held a cardboard sign that said, GOODNESS. Not ALONE. Jacquelin was in her house with strangers. Both Jacquelin and Norah had cut ties with family.

When I reached for *Unless* the second time, Jacquelin was drinking heavily and still living in her own house. About fifty pages in, I realized the story was too close to my reality and I put it back on the shelf.

The house Jacquelin bought, with her now ex-husband John, was on a quiet street with the yard of a Catholic high school at one end. I watched in secret. I didn't tell Jack. I didn't want him to know that I wasn't doing very well at distancing myself from her life, something that he had encouraged me to do. I often checked her street on my way home from visiting with Dad. I'd park if her car was in the driveway. From the little bit of light coming through the window, I suspected she was burning candles. Incense too. She loved both. I could never be sure if she was alone or not. When I called her number, a stranger answered the phone.

"Hello…"

I heard shuffling, and then Jacquelin's harried voice, "Hello, hello?"

I didn't know what to say. I don't exactly know why I called, because the truth was I didn't really want to talk to her. I think I just wanted to hear her voice. Hearing her sound so gruff, worried me.

Might I have said, "Oh, hi there, I'm sitting outside your house stalking you." No, that wouldn't have gone well, and, as I write this now, I'm glad I didn't say that. Truth was, in that particular situation, I had no idea how to talk to my sister. Did I ever? Was there ever a time when I wasn't too careful when I was with Jacquelin?

"Hello?" repeated Jacquelin, impatiently.

She said, "I told you not to answer my phone." I wondered if the stranger heard the reprimand. I hoped he was someone who wasn't prone to strike out.

"Don't pick up the phone again," she added. Then in a softer voice, she said, "It could have been my parents."

Click.

"My parents?" So, she did care. If she could only demonstrate her concern in more constructive ways, I thought. Was Jacquelin attempting to protect them from more disappointment? If so, was she also disappointed in herself? Could she have been empathizing with our elderly parents? At the time I thought that was better than not caring at all.

Did I gain anything from making the call? Peace of mind?

Was it working for me to sit and watch her house from my car? My attempts to see through the curtains of my sister's window was making me feel lonely. I started the engine and drove home. I felt creepy spying on my sister and never did it again.

"What is going on with me? Am I so intrinsically entwined with Jacquelin that I can't let go of her life?" It was really easy for me to think I was always doing the wrong thing. Too bad I didn't just give myself a break. A little more compassion perhaps. At the time it didn't occur to me to think that way. Distress must have been blocking my brain.

Fourteen
Soft Places to Land

September 11, 2017

Some lives are not meant to be long, mine is done, wrote Jacquelin.

After Reverend Ian blessed Jacquelin's body and we had our long chat in the little room at the funeral home, I went home and wrote down a question.

"Who was Jacquelin?"

On the same page I wrote, "She was my sister who was absolutely lovable and when I think of her, I'm going to remember her silhouette with a pony tail down her back, and she's looking west as the sun sets and the day comes to an end."

I pushed forward with funeral arrangements. She had left me to take care of things. Jacquelin knew I would know what to do. I wanted the service to honour her broken heart as much as my own. With Reverend Ian's liturgical direction, I escaped into the task of choosing verses and songs. I invited Julianne to read a verse because I had wanted to honour their friendship. Mel agreed to read too, but at the funeral she was too shaken, and all it took was a silent glance at my cousin Cathy for her to get up and fill the gap. My friend Jan played the piano and Joanne sang two solos. I hoped Jacquelin would like what I came up with. I wanted her to feel love, kindness and compassion. In her note she had written not to suffer for her. Preparing for her final leave taking was what I knew how to do. That part didn't cause me to suffer. It nourished me.

In the throes of shaping Jacquelin's funeral service, I had not lost track of Jack's rounds of chemo. Before his cancer came back the second time in March, 2016, he had chemo administered every two weeks for at least six months. We went to these appointments together. I was there for him as much as for myself. I wanted the full picture. When Jack didn't hear clearly, I picked up missing strands, and he did the same for me. I prepared questions before the appointments and, when we were there, I took notes. Thursdays could be unpredictably long. There was no way I wanted Jack to go through that frustration alone. On Fridays, after he nestled into one of the oversized chairs specifically for chemo, I'd leave to take the dogs into the ravine behind the hospital. This helped alleviate my guilt about Winnie and Zachary getting far fewer walks than they were used to.

Jack mourned his own health, shared in witnessing my father's decline and, before she died, he was deeply troubled about Jacquelin's choices. We were in it together, which helped me cope. In regard to my sister's addiction, he drew on his experience of working in mental health programs. He never questioned how deeply I grieved, about him or Jacquelin. Sometimes he put his big warm hand on my back and left it there until I was finished sobbing. When I went to the first two support circles for survivors of suicide loss, he came with me. He said nothing about my new insistence to sleep at night with the light on. When I announced that he wasn't allowed to hang towels, sheets, or anything else on hooks and doors anymore—because of the vision it created for me—he did his best to remember. When he entered a room too quickly or knocked on a window to let me know he was home, which caused me to jump in freakish terror, he didn't lose patience with me. When I didn't think I could enter into my dad's house alone, he or my friend Joyce came with me.

Residing in my fresh, deep ambiguous grief was a space where it was hard to recognize myself. I had become afraid of the dark. I couldn't sleep. I cried at the drop of hat. I was a grieving sister, daughter, and wife. In my darkest moments, I pushed away thoughts of Jack's death. I went to every oncologist appointment braced in anticipation and couched in prayer.

Fifteen
Jacquelin's Funeral

September 13, 2017

To the congregation in the chapel, I confessed, "There were times when we were at odds. One matter Jacquelin and I did not agree on was what items one should take in the canoe. Admittedly, I had difficulty in understanding why Jacquelin needed to bring her over-stuffed handbag on a short trip to the conservation area. At the same time, she wasn't too happy with my idea about switching paddling positions in the middle of the lake. We were careful not to dump, especially since we had that over-stuffed purse on board. Somehow in the course of our maneuver, and I swear it really was an accident, the flat of my paddle whacked her square in the middle of her forehead. Her response?...First deafening silence...followed by a long sigh...and then, ultimately forgiveness, though it was never explicitly expressed."

I looked into the congregation. People were nodding. They knew her too.

"Jacquelin's quietness befuddled me," I told them. I didn't tell them that it depended on the situation. For example, when she was working at the telecommunications job she once loved, she'd go into great detail about her day.

One of our friends was apt to say, "She's quiet, until she gets started."

From my eulogy, I read, "It wasn't always easy to know what she was thinking. It could feel like she wasn't letting you in and that she didn't want you to know her story." Heads nodded. "If you were fortunate to be invited into the shutter of her camera, even for a little while, you'd know she was bright and articulate; and a good person."

I told them about the last time we spoke. "I had just come from visiting my father at his nursing home. I called Jacquelin to vent my second thoughts about where he was living. She listened and calmly countered my concerns, pointing out pros and cons …the very last conversation we had, helped me take pause."

I've since wondered if Jacquelin realized my gratitude for having helped shift my perspective. Was she listening closely enough? I hope so. Did she not understand that I sometimes needed her?

On the evening of Jacquelin's funeral, three grievers felt compelled to share. Each of the three told me that my sister hated me. How they perceived me and what they had to say, was another place where I did not recognize myself.

The first person to call me on the evening of Jacquelin's funeral, was Anna. When she entered her first year of college and had no place to live, Jacquelin sought permission from my parents for her to live in their home. In the phone call, Anna got around to saying, "She hated you." And in case I didn't get it, she said it again, "She really hated you."

I considered Anna had drunk too much wine and gave her the benefit of the doubt. At the same time, I recalled one of my mother's sayings, "Where there's smoke, there's fire."

"Anna, I'm surprised to hear the word 'hate,'" I said. "No doubt there were times when Jacquelin was frustrated with me. Sisters fight and move on. At least, we did."

Did we? Was there a hint of "something" in Anna's story that I needed to think about more closely? Did the premise of "where there's smoke, there's fire" apply?

Anna had no sisters. Now she has two daughters. When her daughters don't agree, will she recall what I said about sisters and their squabbles?

The other person who felt compelled to tell me how Jacquelin felt about me was Howie. Within hours after the funeral, he wrote me a series of emails. Some of them gushy, others angry. In one note, he said, "Jacquelin hated your guts."

I sent back a brief reply. "We had our moments."

The third person to say Jacquelin hated me was also into the wine, and for that reason, I dismissed the message. Almost.

The statement, "Jacquelin hated you," seemed harsh to pass on after a much-loved sister's death and only a few hours after her funeral. The timing of their missives was curious. Was an alternate message embedded in their words? Was it jealousy? I remembered Howie once told me he got sick and tired of Jacquelin telling him I had a Ph.D. Had any of my callers been projecting their own feelings about me onto to my relationship with my dead sister?

In those moments of unexplained turmoil, I wrote in my journal.

Since I prefer to think in more dialectical terms, I find myself shying away from the absoluteness embedded in the hard use of the word "hate." My intense curiosity about where each person was coming from sustained my quiet patience – in other words, I kept my mouth shut and didn't ask for specifics. To my exhausted self I say: take each perspective in turn. [Journal entry September 13, 2017, the night of Jacquelin's funeral.]

Neither Jacquelin or I had had children. I've always believed my parental-like relationship with Jacquelin fulfilled all maternal instincts, which would possibly explain two things. One, the depth of my organ-love— *splagchnizomai* – that I felt for Jacquelin. And two, since I nurtured both my sisters, I did not have a strong urge to parent a child of my own. I think my nurturing needs had been met. So, when Jacquelin buried herself in alcohol, I grieved the loss of a sister who at times felt like she was my daughter.

One time, when I showed up at my dad's house, Jacquelin literally fled from the room. It felt like she was running away from me. Feeling horrible and sad, I looked at my dad.

"Does Jacquelin hate me?"

His blue eyes locked into my own. His soft tone reached into my soul, "No. Jacquelin doesn't hate you. She just doesn't understand you."

I could see the extent to which Jacquelin resented my dad. He opened his home, his bank accounts and his heart. He wanted her to find a way back to herself. My dad had had a front-row view of Jacquelin's resistance to other people's help, and I suspect he experienced more hostility from her than I did. It seemed the people who tried to help her the most got treated the worst.

The thing is, Jacquelin didn't want to be in his house and she had been living with him long enough to make that message loud and clear. So, when my dad spoke to me about Jacquelin not understanding me, I wondered later if he was including himself. Jacquelin did not understand him. Or me. He knew me and I knew him and that felt good enough. I trusted his wisdom as much as I did his broken heart. It seemed the older and feebler my dad got, the more he became my rock.

In a subdued dinner conversation at his nursing home, table-partner Joan talked about the one son who just visited and how much he was like his older brothers.

"Not like your daughters, eh Dad?"

"No, not like my three daughters." He glanced at Joan. "My daughters are all really different."

I suspect I was seen as the "responsible one." I was named the Power of Attorney and Executor of my parents' wills. Until there was a well-overdue argument among my parents and Jacquelin, I was the only daughter given a key to the cottage. In the summer months I was entrusted to water my mother's beloved tomatoes and oversee their house. If those decisions were made because I was the eldest, it never got discussed. It's just how things went. When my mother was unwell, my father called me. When Jacquelin got into trouble, I was the one they phoned. Did I mind? No. Was it something either of my sisters discussed with me? Nope. Do I think they spoke to one another about the imbalance in my parents' expectations? I can't be sure.

At the end of Jacquelin's life, the tender loving care from the people who surrounded me offset the ridicule and bumpier moments that came in harsh phone calls, nasty emails, and acerbic text messages. Heart-felt cards and notes kept coming, all tucked away now in a large hat box. I grounded myself in my faith. I kept going to church because the people there were prayerful and easy to be with. Plus the woody smell of the sanctuary, grounded me. I went to as many exercise classes as I could. I reached into friendship—long time and new. I embraced the generous qualities of great neighbours who watched out for me, especially when Jack was at his sickest. As well, I was not shy about seeking out the community of support offered by professionals and trained volunteers. The amount of therapy I sought out, worked well for me. The work I did in therapy and the sessions at the Suicide Survivor program guided me in a healing journey. Emotional wellness needed to be the backdrop for my memoir work. But still, when I got down to work, I wrote in circles. I came up with a lengthy list of questions, including, why did everyone in our family tiptoe around Jacquelin? What were we afraid of? From there I awoke to the code of silence in my family. Whenever I offered alternate ways to think about how Jacquelin might resolve a problem, I stepped outside the code and tension erupted.

Sixteen
A Deathtrap

March 17, 2016

I can't sleep. If I could only weep and I might feel better. I need to let go. I need to be. I want to find myself again. I will, once I figure out where to look. God, please show me the way. I am listening. Please help me find me.
[Journal entry, September 9, 2016]

The night after the above journal entry, Jacquelin called. I pressed the phone to my ear and through her raspy words I heard deep sadness, remorse, and fear.

"Are you ready to let me help you?" I wanted her to surrender.

"Yes," she said.

"Where are you? I'll come get you."

"Not tonight. Tomorrow," she said.

"Okay." She was right, it was late. "Tomorrow. I'll come early."

I wrote down the address. When I crawled back into bed, Jack awoke, so I told him about the phone call.

He knew what I wanted to do. "You've been down this road before."

"I need to go get her. I want to help her."

"I know you do. But don't get your hopes up. Be careful..."

"I want to bring her here," I said. "So she can detox."

Jack didn't have a problem with that. We talked about the rules. "No drinking. No smoking inside the house."

I tossed and turned the rest of the night and got up earlier than my six o'clock alarm. Jack slept deep. I didn't wake him. While our dogs, Winnie and Zach, ate in their usual robust fashion, I made coffee.

Heading west on the expressway, I reminded myself to take each step slow. I prayed for a little more help.

I figured Jacquelin would be unorganized, because even in better days she was seldom punctual.

Our wedding came to mind. After the evening rehearsal in the church, Reverend Michael rested his gaze on me. "See you tomorrow and don't be late."

At the time, I thought his comment unnecessary and overstated. "Of course not," I said.

Rides to the church had been prearranged. On the day of the wedding, after everyone left for the church, I waited for Jacquelin and John. They had agreed to pick me up fifteen minutes before the ceremony.

I stood on the front porch and saw my neighbours leaving for the church. They waved and smiled as they left their house. "See you over there!"

Major, my chocolate lab, was beside me while I waited for Jacquelin's car. I called her cell and left a message.

"It's ten to four. I trust you are on your way—"

I drew on my practiced patience and told myself not to panic or weep. The church was a fast ten-minute walk away, but then clad in pumps and an ivory-silk-ankle-length gown, jogging was not in the cards. The thought of calling a cab irked me.

"A cab to my own freaking wedding? You've got to be fucking kidding!"

My patience dwindled, and I chastised myself for giving Jacquelin a time-charged task.

When their vehicle finally appeared, she hurried up the walkway with a platter of fruit.

"Where should I put this?" she asked.

"In the refrigerator…If there's no room, anywhere…please hurry. Jacquelin, we should be there already."

"We'll be okay."

My dad met me at the church steps. "There you are…" His smile helped me to relax.

I let the memory go so I could focus on my turn onto the QEW.

"Anything can happen," I said to myself. "Keep expectations low. Take one minute at a time. Breathe. Pray as needed."

Just like Jacquelin said, the motel was on the south side of The Queensway past Dixon.

My first impression of the rambling two-story building was, "It's a retro-dump."

I parked close to the street and walked across the uneven gravel lot to the door that said, "Office." Inside, a poorly lit lobby with a worn brown carpet. The man behind the counter looked malnourished. He was surrounded by thick plexiglass. So that I could tell him who I was looking for, I bent down to speak through a round metal speaker.

When he spoke, his eyes narrowed. "Room —" His voice was flat.

I heard a sharp buzz, followed by a "click" and he pointed to the door.

"Thank you," I said.

When I entered the drab corridor with the worn soiled carpet the door clicked shut behind me.

On the second floor, I followed a glassed-in walkway that ran the length of the building. The rooms faced Lake Ontario, which on that morning was calm. I had been introduced to the shared-balcony feature in my 1975 urban geography class and could envision the roadside motel as a favoured vacation spot.

Most of the rooms' windows were covered by vertical blinds that were closed tight. A few units were being used for storage. Everything about the motel was outdated and tired. I suspected its tenants, including my sister, were lost and friendless.

According to the skinny guy behind the plexiglass, Jacquelin's room was second from the end. I took a deep breath before I knocked. Then I took another before the next knock, and waited.

It occurred to me that she had bailed already. Then a more horrible thought: she's not okay. I knocked again. The wood on the door was hard under my knuckles.

The next room's door opened just a bit. A woman with shoulder-length blonde hair looked at me.

"Sorry," I whispered.

The door closed and I wondered if she knew what I was up against. Had she spoken to Jacquelin? Maybe she opened the door because she was looking out for my sister.

Knock, knock. Nothing. I tapped on the curtained window. Tap, tap, tap—

A stir inside.

I whispered into the crack of the door. "Jacquelin, it's me."

Movement. My mouth went dry.

"Jacq, it's me, Bev." My heart pumped hard.

I willed her to open the door. "God," I whispered, "let her open the door."

In the door's opened inch, I saw her pale-blue eye. I'd always wanted her to be more cautious.

"It's okay...Jacq. We talked last night. Remember?"

Dressed in a man's golf shirt I could tell she'd just woken up. Siron looked sleepy too. He hadn't barked. What dog doesn't bark when someone knocks on doors and windows? A tired dog.

The smell in the room suggested windows and the door had not been opened. The balled-up bedclothes suggested a hard night.

"Jacq, remember what we talked about on the phone last night? I'm taking you home."

Our call had been around two in the morning. Had I arrived then, I think the motel would have seemed scarier. I suspected my sister was more used to seedy places than I was.

I turned on a lamp. "Let's get your stuff together."

It was difficult to know how long she had been staying in the room. I picked up her jeans from the chair. Under the bed was a shoe. It took more searching to retrieve its mate.

Siron did not move much, which for a puppy, was odd. I noticed dried dog-vomit and diarrhea on the shabby carpet. An empty pizza box sat on the floor. Our dogs sometimes ate pizza crusts too. How much pizza had Siron eaten?

While I attempted to clean up after Siron, Jacquelin shoved a half-filled bottle of white wine into her purse. That's okay, I thought, we'll deal with that later.

I was anxious. I feared she would change her mind, like the other times. Siron wasn't wearing a collar, but I found the red and white leash I had given Jacquelin on one of the times Siron showed up untethered. I figured the little dog had witnessed a lot and he was good to stay close to Jacquelin.

Once belongings were stuffed into the black gym bag, we left the same way I came in because the second floor only had one exit, a dead end.

The morning sky had turned grey and the street in front of the motel was still sleepy.

Jacquelin stopped and fumbled through her purse.

"Jacq, what are you looking for?"

"The key. If I don't give it back, I lose my deposit."

"Can I help?"

"Fuck it…let's just go."

I rushed ahead to unlock the car. Siron jumped into the back seat and Jacquelin pulled the wine bottle out of her purse.

"Your wine has to go into the trunk." I spoke in a soft voice.

"Why?"

"Because we're not supposed to have open liquor in a car."

As casually as I knew how, I attempted to take the bottle from her. Her firm grasp told me she wasn't letting go of the bottle. Physically, she was strong. Especially her arms and hands.

"I have to have it," she said.

"I know. How about we put the wine in the trunk, and at the halfway point…at Sunnyside Park, I'll pull in and you can discreetly take a sip." How she looked at me, made me add this, "Jacq, you have my word. I'll pull over. I promise."

Her hands shook.

I put the wine in the trunk.

As I released the emergency break the clerk's face appeared in the murky window. He creeped me out. The motel was a place where bad things waited to happen.

As I drove, my body felt chilled and I turned on the seat warmer.

"Want some heat?"

"I'm okay."

She wasn't. She looked lost and broken and sad.

"I think you'll find our guestroom cozy. I've got a fluffy robe for you. It was Mom's. You'll have your own bathroom." Jacquelin had had many big fluffy robes and when she lived in her own house, she had three bathrooms. The words I offered seemed futile and out of synch.

"Sounds okay," she said.

I detected appreciation, which I welcomed, because then it might have meant she was closer to how we were raised, not to take other people's hospitality for granted.

"That motel, how did you get there?"

"Mitch brought me there."

"That was good of Howie's dad," I said, figuring there was more of a story.

We sat in my small car but were worlds apart.

A similar wave of gloom sometimes hit after Jack's treatments. After chemo and radiation, Jack curled into the fetal position and stayed that way on the couch for hours. He shivered, and I added more blankets. One of our dogs would lie at his feet. When he opened his eyes, I'd coax him to drink more fluid. Chemo deflated his spirits and when the steroids amped him up, his anger at cancer got loud and clear.

How could I know his world of cancer when I only lived it from the outside? His despondence scared me. That's when I prayed to God and asked for Jack's renewed hope.

Like Jacquelin, Jack stared into space. Both diseases, cancer and alcoholism, shared an intense capacity for an undefined silence that was difficult to navigate. The faraway look screamed fragility and yelled vulnerability. While I was relieved to have Jacquelin sitting safely beside me, I wondered if she felt like my captive. I wondered if Jack ever felt that way?

Beyond cyclists and early-morning dog walkers, Sunnyside Park was vacant. Jacquelin turned her back to the bike lane, and I stood watch. The liquid was her medicine. I figured it was too early for cops but still I was nervous. My promise to her was fulfilled without incident.

At home Jack stood at the counter preparing coffee. When he saw Jacquelin, he stopped to wrap his arms around her.

"Hey kiddo, it is so good to see you."

His embrace made me want to weep with gratitude. When she was less well, hugs weren't readily accepted, so witnessing her melt into Jack's arms brought relief. I wanted her to feel loved and cared for and Jack did that so well. I knew because that's how I felt when he hugged me.

"Jacquelin, you're lucky to have such a good sister. You know that, don't you?"

I suspect he wanted to remind her of my care because he worried I did too much for my sister. When it came to Jacquelin's expression of gratitude, Jack often said she came up short.

"Y-yeah. I do." She glanced in my direction. "T-thanks."

"You're welcome, Jacq. I want to see you feeling yourself again."

She took the wine bottle from her purse and carried it to the couch.

Standing behind the island in the kitchen, Jack said, "We have to talk about that." His stern tone sounded firm. "You're here to detox, right?"

"Yes."

"Okay...so you need to take measured drinks. Once that bottle is empty, no more booze is coming into this house."

Listening, I held my breath. His timbre was measured and while he didn't sound mean, he was clearer than I expected him to be right then. I thought he could be softer. At the time I thought he was a bit over the top. In hindsight, how he handled it was perfect.

Setting clear boundaries with Jacquelin had been hard for me. Even in smaller matters, like when she'd plunk her over-sized purse smack in the middle of my kitchen's island. In light of me having just tidied up for a family gathering, my annoyance would kick in. Clear about my intent— your purse needs to be somewhere else—I'd pause to monitor my exasperation. I was mindful that an expression of anger in my family could easily be interpreted as "someone is being difficult," and since I wanted any gathering to go off without a hitch, I'd learned to pause. Oftentimes my requests to Jacquelin came out sounding tentative. Sometimes she'd move the purse, and other times not. When not, I took the familiar road of least resistance and placed the purse on a chair. When direct with Jacquelin, I'd second-guess myself. I'd ask, "Does it really matter if her gigantic purse is cluttering my workspace?" Answer: "Yes." Was it worth asking her to remove it? It would depend on how much energy I had.

I didn't want to be perceived as an autocrat. When Jacquelin was unwell, having to be direct included telling her what to do, something I didn't relish. But I couldn't not take the responsibility. Still, talking with Jacquelin was often fraught because I couldn't communicate with her as I normally would. Had it always been this way? When she was five, ten, and fifteen, I knew her better. Even in her thirties. But at forty-something and into her early fifties, I unknowingly fell out of knowing my sister. Does my struggle resonate with a loving parent who wonders and worries about the future of their adult child?

In his clearest of terms, Jack outlined the boundaries to Jacquelin. It was good that he was several hours away from chemo. I was relieved not to be doing it alone.

"It's up to you, Jacquelin," he said. "Pace yourself and you won't get into trouble."

I offered her our guest room with a private bathroom. I suggested a soak in the tub. During the time she stayed with us, however, she planted herself on our red leather couch. She sat there, and surrounded by all of her stuff, she slept. I let it go. What I told myself was this: it's okay. It's what needs to happen right now. Stuff doesn't matter. She matters.

On one of the mornings during that stay, friends of Jack's who were anxious to check in on him, dropped in for coffee. Jacquelin had met them before and I embraced their impromptu visit as a miracle. Why? Because each person offered Jacquelin their encouragement and compassion. No one judged her. I wanted her to notice their acceptance of her as much as I did.

Over strong coffee and toasted bagels, Christina mentioned she was on her way to give an AA talk at a downtown women's shelter and invited Jacquelin to come along. To my amazement, Jacquelin agreed. Another miracle? Christina had quietly revealed to Jack that she was looking forward to sponsoring a new female AA member and I was hoping Jacquelin would be the one.

Around the notion of getting a sponsor, I heard from Christina that Jacquelin would "think about it." From experience I knew what she meant and the music in my ears dampened. Jacquelin believed her problems weren't as dire as Christina's and therefore didn't require what AA had to offer. I wanted my sister to extrapolate meaning from Christina's experience of acquiring a less chaotic life—a sober life. Fully aware that self-help groups, especially AA, aren't for everyone, I empathized with Jacquelin's hesitancy.

I understood the power of sponsorship in AA and assumed it needed to hold the qualities of a good friendship but with a different set of boundaries. I pictured Jacquelin thriving with a mentor, someone who could be a sounding-board and a gentle guide who would tell her what they saw. I had hoped Jacquelin would attentively listen with more patience to someone other than me.

Jacquelin had a desire to emulate the life Melody lived. She valued Mel's business sense and her administrative position with its authority, autonomy, and abundant salary. Mel made it look easy.

"Yes Jacq," I'd said, "but those privileges evolved from many years of hard work."

Not seeing it that way, Jacquelin called Melody for advice. From my perspective Jacquelin's pattern of drinking had escalated well beyond "how to be a social drinker." When I'd learned that Jacquelin had been advised by Melody on how to drink more responsibly, I was livid. Melody and I quarreled. I thought Jacquelin needed a serious intervention. She was an alcoholic and could no longer drink safely. Whatever Jacquelin required was more than what her two older sisters could say or do.

After seventy hours of detoxing at our house, I mentioned a hopeful next step.

"Jacquelin, Dad said he'll pay for rehab."

I don't recall a response. Note to self: timing is everything. I'm not sure if she remembered the night before when she'd agreed to go to into rehab. My heart sang when she had said it.

Prior to picking Jacquelin up at the motel, I'd had a wonderfully supportive conversation with one of the counsellors at a rehabilitation centre for women with addictions.

"I can hear what you're doing for your sister," she said. "But what about you? Are you also taking care of yourself?"

Was I taking care of myself? I knew the importance of her question. In some ways, "yes." Someone had reminded me to drink lots of water, so I did. Since I was focused on Jack's and my father's nutrition, I was mindful of my own, and was eating well. I was fortunate to have a couple of neighbours who dropped off food. When Jack was well enough, we went to our favourite pub. Comfort food was always on the menu. I wasn't getting enough sleep, in part because I was drinking too much coffee.

The addictions counsellor on the other end of a phone line had asked the right question. I felt teary and gulped down my emotions. If she noticed, she didn't say but I'm pretty sure she would have understood that too. The phone call closed with optimism when I said I hoped she would have a chance to work with my sister.

"Dad, a few years ago I attended a fundraiser at Hope Place. I was really impressed. It was lovely. Anyway, I called them, and they have a bed for Jacquelin. I sense the people who work there, love what they do."

It felt like we were getting closer to getting her help. Note to self: breathe. Keep expectations in check. I needed to constantly remind myself that plans could get interrupted. There was something else I needed to be thinking about: it was all up to Jacquelin. Breathe deep.

In the early morning hours of the second day of detoxing at our house, Jacquelin's murmuring voice woke me. I heard her talking to someone. My stomach clenched. I got up and listened from the top of the stairwell. Her talking was non-stop. By the time I reached the bottom stair, I'd considered two possibilities: she was speaking to on-and-off-boyfriend and planning a getaway like she did before, or she was "dialing a bottle."

Not wanting to startle her, I crept along the hallway. She was sitting up straight on the couch and was alone. She wasn't on the phone.

"Jacquelin?"

There was no acknowledgment. She didn't look at me. She focused on her sweater. She picked at her arms. She was looking for something. Like she was searching for pieces of lint or bugs or something.

"Jacquelin?"

She muttered words, but not to me. Gibberish.

I rushed to the staircase and called up. "Jack, I need your help."

"What's happening?"

"Jacquelin. She's talking to herself and she's not responding to me."

"She might be having a seizure." He was calm. He'd seen them before—students in his mental health program and guys in the detox where he worked at the beginning of his career.

"I'm calling 911," I said.

"Yep. Good idea."

I held my sister like a baby in my arms. She let me. I was afraid she was going to die.

Later, I learned people don't usually die from seizures, unless they bump their heads badly, but I'd never witnessed one before so I didn't know. It was frightening. She felt as light as my mother when she collapsed in my arms three years earlier.

I had a person from the emergency dispatch on speaker phone. I described the situation.

"She's rocking back and forth. Picking at her skin...Incoherent. She's been weaning herself off alcohol...Around seventy-two hours."

"Sounds like a seizure. Get her onto the floor...away from anything hard..."

I laid Jacquelin on her side. Jack put the dogs away and stood at the door and watched for the ambulance. When the paramedics arrived, he directed them into our living room.

Terrified, I left her side so the paramedics could to do their work. After they treated her, she sat back on the couch. One paramedic spotted a travel-size bottle of Scope. I'd not seen it there before and I didn't know whether it was alcohol-free.

"That!" Pointing, he looked at me with disgust. "You should have put that away."

It hadn't occurred to me to search my sister.

"We'll be taking her to Sunnybrook." His tone was laced with judgement.

I'm not sure if Jacquelin noticed how he spoke, but I did. I was shocked. I was also taken aback I'd missed the mouthwash.

Hardly looking at her, he said, "You can walk to the truck." His sharp edgy voice was memorable. So, this is how alcoholics get treated. Not like other sick people. Not like people with cancer.

After Jacquelin was gone, I restored our living room to its normal state. I drank coffee. I felt depleted, exhausted, and a little stunned. It took me a while to settle down. She had scared me.

Like with my mom, I said nothing about going into the ambulance with Jacquelin or following in my car. I thought they would keep her, and there wasn't a need for me.

A short time later, Jacquelin called to say she was ready to leave the hospital. I thought there would be an intervention and that she would get help. Her time in the hospital would have been a break for me, a respite. I wanted help for her and me.

Jacquelin appeared near the nursing station before I had time to tell the nurse who I was looking for. My sister clutched a pamphlet and several pieces of rumpled paper. She didn't speak. She hardly looked at me. She looked tense and angry.

How the nurse followed her with her eyes, bothered me. The same way as it bothered me with the paramedic who had spoken to her earlier.

I leaned over the counter so I could scold the nurse. "She's not a bad person. She's unwell and we're trying to help her get better."

Had Jacquelin been a challenging patient and had I said too much to the nurse? In this journey, there's lots of room for second-guessing. In those moments, I had to work hard from drowning in ambivalence. Even now, I kept telling myself this means trusting the meaning I make of what I see and hear around me. Most of all, I worked hard not to ignore my intuition.

I caught up to Jacquelin. "My car is just outside the emergency department."

With legs longer than mine, she picked up the pace, and I recognized her extra effort to dismiss me and leave me in her dust. At the security desk, still in her shadow, she reached for a couple of tissues. Or so I thought. Instead she swiped the entire box off the table and put it into her purse.

The security person hadn't seen. Would it have mattered? To me it did.

Her belligerence sickened me. I knew what she was saying: "Fuck you." For my benefit? Likely. Had the nurse behind the counter witnessed some of the same? At the time, whatever pain and confusion Jacquelin was acting out, I knew there was no right way to address it. What worked was: let it go.

As she opened the car door, she said, "Why did you have to go and call 911?"

"Because you were having a seizure, that's why."

"Well," she hissed, "now they're probably going to take my licence away."

The penny dropped: someone at the hospital had spoken to her about a medical suspension on her driving licence and she was pissed off at me.

They didn't. She didn't lose her licence. I suspect the paperwork got lost.

Seventeen
More Wise Women

September 28, 2017

Thanks to Betty-Lynn from Saskatoon, cognitive behavioural therapist, Dr. Eilenna Denisoff of Toronto, was expecting my call. When she asked how I was doing I told her sleep wasn't coming easily, and to cope, I was keeping busy with Jacquelin's affairs, spending time with my father who was adjusting to a nursing home, and doing my best to support my husband who was battling stage four lung cancer.

"Whew. You certainly have a lot on your plate," she said at the end of our introductory conversation. "Watch the wine."

I knew she was the woman I wanted to work with.

Fourteen days after Jacquelin's funeral, I went to Dr. Denisoff's practice in a modern-glass building on University Avenue near Adelaide Street. I gave myself an hour to travel on the Leaside bus to the St. Clair Subway and then take the southbound train to St. Patrick.

When I got onto the crowded car, it was a relief to spot a vacant seat. I yearned to sit, close my eyes and let my mind drift. When I opened them, I was alarmed to see a woman with a noose around her neck. She was hanging from the train's over-head handrail. I'm not sure if the person sitting beside me heard my gasp. My mind filled with horror and I jerked away as fast as I could. I squeezed my eyes shut and nestled my face in my hands. I concentrated on my breathing to slow my racing heart. Determined not to be frightened, I opened my eyes and looked to the right. There was the attractive young South Asian woman holding the handrail over her head. To understand that earlier stark image, I studied how her arm reached up and tilted her head to one side. Relieved, I breathed deep and waited in anticipation for my stop.

After my brisk walk along University, I sat on a leather sofa in a stylish waiting room with lots of abstract art on the walls. I held a clip board on my lap and answered questions on the intake form. Right on time, Dr. Denisoff escorted me past art-filled walls to her office where I plunked my fatigued body into a chair. Behind me was a large pane of glass capturing Toronto's south vista from eleven floors up. It was the view I did not notice until many months later when I paused, finally free of my trauma, to look out the window of her corner office.

I told Dr. Denisoff about the horrifying image of the young South Asian woman in the subway. "I'm a mess," I said. "A wreck."

In another early session, I had told her about what my brain did when my eye caught something Jack had hung on a hook and over a door. I proudly told her my new house rule: "no hanging things on hooks or doors." She said that it had to be okay for Jack to hang sheets, towels, and whatever else on wall hooks and doors. She helped me understand that I was prolonging the image. My brain had some unlearning to do. It's not Jacquelin, she said. I needed to face a coat, a towel or a blanket hung over the door.

She helped me understand why I started to panic when I walked from a room with light into one that was dark. That's how it was on the night I found Jacquelin, when I walked through a brightly lit house into the dimly lit room where I found her. I was afraid the image of Jacquelin would re-emerge. Therefore, when transitioning from a room with light to one that was dark, I adopted new strategies, including talking to myself and doing a lot of deep breathing.

To trick my brain, I reached for the light switch from the hallway. The thought of stepping into a dark room scared me and I didn't want to trigger my grief. To cope, I turned on the light *before* I stepped in. Years earlier, my dad had installed two-way switches and I was thankful because they helped with this little trick on my brain. However, when

I told Dr. Denisoff about my coping strategies, she pointed out that I wasn't doing myself any favours. It took some time to trust that I could transition into the dark without a panic attack. I had to work at remembering what Dr. Denisoff had said about retraining my brain. I actually had to practice walking into dark rooms. Did I feel flutters in my stomach? You bet, lots of them. But they are fewer now.

Eighteen
Me As Outlier

Summer 1999

In preparation for the celebration of my parent's fiftieth wedding anniversary I became befuddled by the outcome of Jacquelin's insistence of being the one to prepare the PowerPoint presentation with pictures. She had dismissed my technical know-how and said she would do the scanning. Appreciative of her taking on the task, I handed over a box of selected photographs and my new scanner which was still sealed in its box.

The party was on Saturday August, 19, 1999, and the weather was perfect. My mother had always spoken lovingly about her Trousseau Tea, so I mimicked it. I also borrowed a mannequin stand to exhibit her wedding dress. Tables for lunch were arranged in my parents' backyard under the trees.

The slide presentation was a surprise for everyone, and I looked forward to how Jacquelin would choreograph the box of photographs. I knew scanning could take a fair bit of time, so in days prior to the event I offered my help.

"Got it covered, Beverley. Quit worrying." In other words, "Go away and let me do things my way."

A screen and projector had been strategically placed in the shade of the yard and the intrigue among guests filled the air.

At the end of my speech, I said, "Thanks to Jacquelin's work behind the scenes, I'm pleased to tell you that we have a special presentation."

Jacquelin's hands shook as she poured a generous amount of Grand Marnier into a short glass. At the same time, one of my aunts whispered, "Oh, I'm so looking forward to this."

Me too, but I was unsure what sense to make of the tremor in Jacquelin's hands.

When she pressed the enter key a lovely image appeared on the screen. My parents were standing outside the doors of the church where they were married in 1949. My mother's white satin dress, with lace, fit perfectly. She held a bouquet of twelve long-stem red roses. Short brown hair framed her radiant face. My father, dressed in a dark suit, looked incredibly handsome.

That was it. All done. One photograph onto one slide. Just one. From all of the pictures I'd given her—forty or fifty in all shapes and sizes—she had picked only one. Presentation over. Jacquelin took up her glass and sat down.

Yikes, I thought. What the hell just happened?

I stood and smiled into the crowd. "Thank you very much, Jacquelin. . . .I've always loved that picture of Mom and Dad. . .Thank you for sharing. . .That was great. . ." I reminded the guests, "Dancing will be on the deck in a little while. . .Perhaps you'd like another drink from the bar. . .Coffee or tea. . .Or more dessert. . ."

Jacquelin's glass was empty. She didn't look at me. Had she, I'm not sure what she would have said. "I'm embarrassed? I'm sorry?" Not a word.

It wasn't the time, but later if I were to have said anything, it would have been, "I wanted to help you. . .Why didn't you let me help you?"

Sometime after I shared my concern with my parents. "Coming across as an instant expert is going to get her into trouble."

My father said nothing and my mother told me to forget about it.

Days passed before I phoned Jacquelin. I left a message, "I'll come by and pick up the scanner. I need it for work."

I left messages on voicemail, which told me my calls were screened.

To my parents, I said, "When you see her, would you please ask her to return the scanner?"

My pleas fell into a dead zone. Eventually, I earned the nick-name, "Miss Pain-in-the-Ass-Scanner," and people in my family thought that was pretty funny.

"Ha, ha. Hilarious," I said to Jack.

Persistent as I was, I did eventually get a scanner back but not the one I bought. The scanner returned to me didn't work, so I disposed of it. Blinded by exasperation, I had no capacity to fathom whatever happened to my brand-new machine, or why I was treated so badly. It was crazy-making.

***

In 2001 at the Toronto Western Hospital, Dr. W removed a benign tumor that was leaning on my bowel and growing into my spine. While I recovered at home after a surgery, my doctoral advisor, Dr. MC, was kind enough to loan me one of the university's laptops. The laptop, loaded with research software and other programs, was in topnotch shape.

Once I was catheter free and able to move around with ease, Jack thought cottage time would do us both some good. I was happy when Jacquelin decided to join us. At that time, she had been laid off from her job at Bell and was enrolled in an intensive Microsoft program at a community college. She planned to complete some course work over the weekend.

"Sounds good to me," I said.

I expected a low-key weekend and was looking forward to revisiting my thesis research. That's why I took the laptop.

In the wee hours of the first morning, I was awoken by unfamiliar noises of pinging and ponging. I got up and followed the sounds. In the dining room was my maternal grandmother's dining set, which was a gift from her oldest son when he returned from the Japanese War camp.

The university's laptop—holding all of the project-research files that I had coded for my doctoral advisor's research team—was on the table in front of where Jacquelin sat.

Ping. Pong.

She had accessed the laptop without my permission, but worse than that, she had disassembled the entire computer. Parts and pieces—the guts of it—covered the expansive top of the dining table. It was very early in the morning, and I had to check if I were awake. It would have been better if it had been a dream. Even a nightmare. It wasn't.

"Jacquelin...What have you done to that computer?"

The research programs—my advisor's precious research—and all of the coding in files I had done, were scattered across the tabletop. Hours and hours of back-straining work. Just like nine hours of face-down surgery on my back where I was disassembled, so was the project's coded research, my future. I considered what this could mean to the completion of my dissertation. Flooded with dread, I pictured being in my advisor's dreary book-filled office and the look of disgust on his face.

"Jacquelin, what have you done?"

Her gaze moved from the three-ring binder to clusters of computer chips and other black plastic parts on the table.

"Jacquelin, you didn't ask me if you could use the computer. Never mind take it apart...It's not even mine..."

She moved the black pieces of plastic like she would if playing a game of chess.

"I hope you know how to put that thing back together, because—"

She looked at me. "Don't worry. I know what I'm doing."

I tried to measure the irresponsibility and thoughtlessness of her actions. I attempted to evaluate the flat tone of her voice. "It's an assignment for the Microsoft training course I'm taking at—."

"Yeah but—"

"Don't worry Beverley, I know what I'm doing."

"Jacquelin, this computer has to go back together exactly the way you found it. There's software on it that's complicated…I've got my thesis research saved on a zip drive, but there's research software…"

I could hardly breathe.

When I fully recovered from my surgery, I went back to the university and I returned the laptop. A few days later, my advisor's technical expert stood beside my work station.

"That laptop you borrowed?"

"Yes?" My stomach flipped like it does when I fear what's coming.

"It's been stripped," he said.

I looked at him in horror. "I don't know why that would have happened."

Fortunately, the technician was a person of few words and walked away perhaps not knowing what to say. He couldn't have been any more befuddled than I felt. I'd taken my sister's word when she said the computer was back together. It hadn't occurred to me she wasn't telling the truth. I also didn't know if the condition of the laptop had been reported to my supervisor.

The project was about lives lived in a particular classroom. Jacquelin had access to private information, research not yet published. Had I told my advisor the truth I would have had to convince him my sister wasn't curious about other people's lives. (Generally, she wasn't.) However, the point was this: I left the computer unattended and in the strictest of protocol, the research should have been under lock and key.

Had I told the true story my professor might not have felt compassion toward my sister or me.

Did I have compassion for Jacquelin? Yes. She took apart the computer because she had been running scared. Or was she scared to death and trying to prove something to herself? I suspect she was reeling in regret that she had lost a secure and well-paying job. I recognized the despair in her eyes. She held her lips tight. The look resembled the fear I saw in the faces of previous students. Whenever I talked about their struggles and stories of success to Jacquelin—hoping she would take a lesson from my telling—she didn't listen.

"I'm not like your students, Beverley."

In part, the work I did with students who had troubles not dissimilar to Jacquelin's, readied me for my journey with my sister. I have been grateful for how my earlier teaching life informed my path. It was never apparent that she connected with the stories I told. She was right, she wasn't my student. However, sometimes she was like the most troubled of them. But not one of them ever took my computer apart.

I felt compassion for Jacquelin but I didn't hold the same for myself. At the time I didn't recognize that, but now I see it.

After Dr. Denisoff listened to my stories, she said there was a good possibility Jacquelin was bipolar. If she was right, at what point in my sister's life did the disease show up?

Looking back, Jacquelin felt free to enter into my private sphere. I don't suggest this had anything to do with being bipolar or not. But how did she know to do that? What messages had she received? Had my family's avoidance of arguing with her and tiptoeing through her silences, been shaping factors?

As my stories about my sister came together, I noticed Jacquelin presented herself as having fast and unexamined solutions to complex problems. She gave off the impression she knew how to do something when she didn't. I am reminded of this when I visualize the assigned pile of thick-training binders for her new job. The binders remained unopened over the weekend before the training's start date.

I nudged her to get to the reading. She scoffed. That worried me. Her over-confidence bothered me. When my sister posed herself as an expert—like she did with the scanner and then again with the laptop—my concern deepened. I was not surprised to learn that Jacquelin did not successfully complete her Microsoft training program for her new job.

***

I'm not sure if Jacquelin forgave my honest feelings about how she ended her marriage. My sister was displeased with my empathy for her husband. In Jacquelin's mind, it was plain and simple—I had taken her husband's side.

I didn't tell her or my mother—deception on my part—about our one time visit with my ex-brother-in-law in his new home. I'm pretty sure Jack's and my visit would have been construed by my mother as siding with my ex-brother-in-law and more betrayal of Jacquelin.

Jacquelin mirrored my mother's perception of black and white on issues. Grey was the colour I could see, and that often left me feeling the outlier. What I wanted was for my sister to be more like me and less like my mother.

Jacquelin and I were estranged for quite some time after her split, and I continued to be an outlier in the family. That's why when my parents popped over to our house for a visit, I didn't know what was going on in Jacquelin's life. They told me as I served coffee on the front porch.

"We've got good news," said my mother.

As she spoke, her face appeared sheepish. My mother was no stranger to the turbulence between her two daughters. She knew we hadn't spoken in months. I suspected my mom was well aware of my disappointment. I didn't like feeling like an outsider.

"Jacquelin is engaged," she said.

My mother wanted each of her daughters to have a man in her life, a husband. Marriage was a measure of success.

"Really? Who is she engaged to?" I tried to tone down the sarcasm in my voice.

"His name is Carl. His family owns a horse farm."

"Yeah? How long has she known him?" and after that answer, I said, "Seems a bit quick to be engaged."

Did I sense Jacquelin was navigating her way into a disaster-based relationship? Did my mother pick up on my disgust? Was that helpful to my relationship with my mother?

Eventually Jack and I were invited over to Jacquelin's house to meet the fiancé. On the way home, Jack was quiet.

"What do you think of the new guy?"

"Obsequious. Smarmy."

"Really?"

When I asked Jack to say more, he said, "I've got a bad feeling. I didn't want to shake his hand."

Trusting Jack's instincts, my stomach churned. "Oh dear—"

"Where'd she meet him?"

"He's the cousin of a really good friend." I took a breath. "A set-up from a trusted friend whom you know and wants the best for you can be confusing," I said.

"Did she seem happy to you?" he asked.

"Couldn't tell…she was really hyper." And there was wine involved, maybe too much.

"Yeah," said Jack, "Jacquelin's either wall paper or a non-stop chatterer." We talked about social anxiety and how it shows up.

"Tonight, she was loud and obnoxious. Could have been the booze."

"Yeah, or maybe smarmy is catching," said Jack with a cough.

On the short drive, we talked about how complex and unpredictable some people could be.

"As you've come to know, the relationships with each of my sisters are different but equally complex. Would you agree?"

"Oh yeah!"

Sometimes when Jack and I talked about my siblings, he expressed gratitude for being an only child. This was one of those times.

I've always told him that I'm happy to have sisters. "It's not always been complicated. Remember at the cottage how we'd push back the furniture to make room to dance and sing out loud together?"

"Yeah—"

"I think we need to dance more."

"That would be good," he said, parking his jeep in front of our house.

Months later, Mel confirmed that Carl had been physically and emotionally violent towards our sister. Jack had been on to something, and my intuition didn't fail me either. But what good did our inner-knowing do? No one was listening. When the relationship ended sometime in early spring, Jacquelin claimed to love him and miss him deeply.

What I did not appreciate about the guy was that after she knew him, she acquired a taste for whiskey. About ten years earlier, Jacquelin hardly took a drink.

Nineteen
Support, Confrontation, and, the Fat Lil' Book

October 2017

My therapy sessions with Dr. Denisoff dovetailed with two of the drop-in meetings with Alex and the eight-week program I enrolled in at the Crisis and Distress Centre. The program was designed specifically for people who had lost a loved-one to death by suicide or homicide. Liz and Edgar, two volunteer counsellors, both survivors with an abundance of time behind them working through their own grief, gently supported me through the early days of coming to terms with my loss.

The first time I met Liz and Edgar was in an office at a meandering and hideous-looking 1970s-style plaza in North York. I liked it better when our meetings were held in Liz's home. She did too, but for Edgar it meant a longer drive into the city. So, there was a compromise and the meetings were divided between the two places. When we met in Liz's home, Edgar and she sat across from me on the French Provincial couch. The wingback chair beside the fireplace was reserved for me. Liz's seven-year-old white lab and I liked one another, and she sat by my feet. Sunlight shone through the leaded glass and I was surrounded by Liz's beautiful antiques. In the dreary North York office, it felt like being in a dark hole.

Time spent with them was powerfully warm, kind, generous, and all embracing. We met eight times, and I looked forward to each session. I thought I'd remember all of what we talked about but I can't be sure if I have. I did not journal but my memory holds the intensity. The essence of my time with Liz and Edgar was unconditional care and acceptance. The pace was slow and right. When I was there, I let go. I let them help me. Not once were my bad dreams and scary memories minimized. They guided me to talk about the past, but not dwell there.

When they asked how I was coping, I told them about my Fat Lil' Notebook. For almost eleven months I carried it—three-by-two inches in size with wire-spiral binding— in my purse. It was handy to keep track of tasks and it later assisted my full-murky brain with specific dates, tasks, and events. I did a lot of flipping through the dog-eared pages of that Fat Lil' book.

Where I wrote, "Call Betty D," I was reminded of two days of watching Jack mutely staring into space. I called his long-time friend Betty for help. Immediately after our conversation, she phoned his cell to tell him get off his ass and stop isolating. I liked Betty's style, and her abrupt directive made Jack laugh. I laughed too.

Their conversation left me free to take Aarif— a gay-man refugee who had narrowly escaped persecution in Iran and whom my church was helping—shopping. He needed winter boots, his first pair. On our way to Mark's Work Warehouse, a thirty-something cop with red hair pulled me over. Unbeknownst to me, my licence sticker had expired six months ago. The fine was hefty, but worse was knowing I'd just acquired another task. Angry with myself, I knew full well I'd shirked my responsibilities. This was one sign that I'd lost track of taking care of myself in the throes of watching out for others, whether they wanted me there or not.

Feeling pissed off with myself added to my tiredness. To catch a breath, I leaned my forehead against the steering wheel. Aarif sat beside me in the front seat. He touched my shoulder and his tenderness made me weep. I supposed those tears had been nearing the surface because the warmth from his big hand on my shoulder felt too compassionate to bear.

"Bev, it is okay," said Aarif, "do not worry, everything is going to be okay."

"You're right," I said. "Things will work out."

From the side of the car the cop hadn't moved, though he may have looked away. The cynic in me wondered if he'd pulled me over because a dark-skinned man was beside me in the front seat. I pushed hard to dismiss the thought. I considered telling the officer why I might have forgotten to purchase the sticker—Jack's cancer, my mother's recent death, my sad and unwell father, and my attempts at saving a raging youngest sister.

I turned the ticket over and saw that I had acquired a three-hundred-and-fifty-dollar fine. The cop pointed to the place to add a checkmark if I wanted to go to court and protest the offense. How helpful, I thought. (Months later, I provided proof of my renewed sticker. The entire fine was dismissed.)

Throughout the next two-hundred or so pages of my Fat Lil' Notebook were "To Do" lists. Flipping the pages, I saw my notation about my dad's first botched nursing home experience. On the page, I wrote:

- morning blood sugar up from 15.2
- fever
- 9:30 a.m. fall from bed—stiffened in the arms of PSW, fell, hit arm on chair, broke skin
- EMS reported: dehydrated; (ear) temperature—38; At hospital (underarm) 36.6
- Catheter—not changed
- EMS—suspected sepsis

After the debacle, I had to fight to get my dad back into the hospital that had pretty much forced his premature discharge. I remember being in combat mode.

***

Liz and Edgar acknowledged the turmoil in my life beyond my sister's tragic death. I was grateful that they embraced all of me. They were interested in knowing about Jack and my family. They asked about

Mel, and I told them she was talking with a counsellor, but on the phone.

"Next time you come, bring us some pictures," said Liz.

The week after, I passed Liz the picture of Jack. She held it and leaned over to show Edgar. As she handed the picture back, her eyes smiled.

"Your husband is very handsome."

I agreed and Edgar chuckled. I had the feeling he expected her to say that and I thought how fortunate I was, that they liked each other.

She picked up the picture of Jacquelin and said, "She was a very attractive woman."

"Yes. She was."

They asked me about my relationship with Jacquelin. I told them I remembered when she was born and that it was love at first sight. I talked about Melody being a robust five-year-old, and that may have been why my mother embraced my help with both of my sisters.

"What about you?" asked Edgar. "What kind of child were you?"

"Anyone who knew me said I was the quiet one. My mother's well-behaved child," I said with a chuckle.

I shared my memory about my kindergarten class and the blue and white playhouse inside the classroom with matching window boxes. I thought the house was magical and remember waiting in anticipation for Miss D to say, "Beverley, today it's your turn to play inside the house."

"She never did."

Liz gasped. "How unkind."

"Yeah well, I got over it." I laughed. I pictured Miss D on the piano bench and recall thin grey hair knotted into a bun at the nape of her neck. Her eyes were dull, and never did I hear her laugh. She had a scowl.

"Now I wonder, was she sad, tired, or burned out?"

"What was kindergarten like for Jacquelin?" asked Edgar.

"I don't think I ever knew. At the time I was grappling with how to fit into grade twelve in an unfamiliar high school that was different from the one I'd left behind."

Victoria Park Secondary was newer and larger. It didn't have that old musty smell and when I walked up the stairs, they didn't squeak. Unlike Runnymede Collegiate, none of the teachers knew anything about my parents or their siblings, or about me. I had no history with my new school.

When my family moved to Toronto's east end, my mother walked Jacquelin to kindergarten class in the school down the street. That left Mel, who was in grade seven, to register herself at her new junior high. I suppose it didn't occur to my mother to ask me to help out. Perhaps she didn't want me to miss any school time. Years later, Mel told me there was a lot of fuss at the junior high's registration desk, and, because she arrived without a parent, it was assumed she was a "special needs kid." That's why they registered Mel in a special after-school group.

"Why didn't you tell them your mother was taking care of her toddler?"

"Because I didn't want them to take me out of that group. I liked the teacher and those kids were a lot of fun!"

I'm not sure if Jacquelin had any favourite teachers. In grades one, two, or three, was there a special friend? I think so. Leanne. By the time Jacquelin was in grade two, I was entering first-year university. When she was in grade three, I'd already moved into residence and when she was in grades four and five, I was thinking I'd met the love of my life and was engaged to be married. At the beginning of her life, I minded her closely, and then after she went to school our paths grew apart. It was the natural consequence of an eleven-year age difference. Living in different physical spaces brings distance and takes people away from one another. I didn't even hear second-hand stories about her elementary years.

My weekly therapy sessions with Dr. Denisoff and talks with Liz and Edgar provoked lots of deep reflection about who I was in Jacquelin's life and how aspects of that role changed over time. Those conversations helped me explore who I was in my own life and I appreciated their constant reminder to be as present for myself as I was for others.

Twenty
A Writing Assignment Becomes a Treasure

June 1978

After my dad got settled in his nursing home, I was preparing his house to sell it. That is when I discovered four dusty boxes that belonged to Jacquelin in my father's basement. When I looked inside, I knew it had the potential of filling the four-year-time gap in her life.

Two boxes contained an extensive collection of comic books—Archie and Veronica and super-hero types. Another box held cards and letters. The fourth box contained some of Jacquelin's writing dating back to 1978. She had saved a hand-written, single-spaced school-book report on Timothy Findley's *The Wars*, with the grade and the teacher's scrawled notations in red ink.

"Very clear writing..." and the grade was B+.

When I talked about the books in my session at Liz's house, Edgar smiled and said, "You found a real treasure."

"Yes, and better, were two small novels in authentic book format including a summary, title page, table of contents, and acknowledgements. I like that her teacher had designed such a comprehensive assignment. Both book covers were made from the wallpaper in my sisters' bedrooms."

Inside the jacket of *The Runaway Plan*, was the synopsis:

A girl who is fed up with her home and family suddenly runs off to a place called Greenwich. She ends up in a dungeon. Read how this summer holiday turned out to be a nightmare.

On the first page, Jacquelin wrote,

I am Cary Westly, laying on my bed, staring at the ceiling – bored as usual.

"Cary!" my mother yelled from downstairs. "Cary?" she said again, only louder. "Cary," she screamed at the top of her lungs.

"What?" I screamed, just coming out of a daze.

"Get down here right now for supper!"

"All right, all right."

"When I got downstairs and was seated at the table, my parents started nagging me. First, they said that I was being too mouthy. Then they said that I couldn't go to the dance with my friends, at the school on Thursday. And they went on and on about everything I had ever done wrong."

I was struck by the opening chapter's reflection on how my mother managed her teenage daughter's lethargy. Cary, the novel's protagonist, has a snappy wit that riles her mother. The autobiographical thread rang true, and I could almost hear my mother enunciate the word, "mouthy."

Jacquelin's bio, accompanied by a picture, was inside the back flap.

About the Author

My name is Jackie Brewer and I am twelve years old. I was born in Toronto in the year 1966. I love to water ski, swim and play tennis, and I also love to write stories.

I had no idea she played tennis and I had no memory of her on water skis. I recall her driving the boat for other people. Her penchant to work as a proposal writer might have been part of an earlier dream of being a writer.

On the cover of the second novel, *Shiver*, her name was spelled Jacqueline, with an "e." It's worth noting that my mother's name is Jacqueline with an "e." Mel was listed as the illustrator, so I thought she might have some insight into the spelling error. I called her up to poke at her memory.

"Mel, you're acknowledged by as the illustrator in little novel Jacquelin wrote."

"I am?"

I thought there was a chance Mel might know the teacher who assigned the project, L. Clark. She didn't.

"Someone mistakenly put an 'e' on the end of Jacquelin's name," I said.

Quick to retort, she said, "It wasn't me. I wouldn't spell my sister's name wrong."

"Did you know Jacquelin played tennis?"

"No and I don't think she liked to swim either."

"She swam when the water was warm," I said.

I told Mel about my lengthy swims with Jacquelin around the island. How did she not know that? Were we three sisters who didn't know each other's lives?

When I summarized Jacquelin's stories, Mel recognized the dynamic between protagonist Cary and her nagging parent, and she grumbled about the school dances she didn't go to because of having to babysit Jacquelin.

In *Running Away*, Jacquelin describes how Cary and her new friend Sara manage to outsmart two men chasing them through tunnels underneath a house that was about to burst into flames.

I came up behind him and hit him as hard as I could. When he had fallen to the ground, I searched his pockets for keys.

"I found them," I said quietly. I slipped my hand between the bars and put the key in the lock and opened the door…

Then we crept along the path she showed us. I looked at my watch and we only had five minutes left before they would set the old place on fire. There was tunnel after tunnel. We only had half a minute left. We were near the entrance, when we could smell smoke. The tunnel started to cave in so we were blocked. We had to follow another path.

And they did find a way out. Jacquelin's characters get to a phone in a small shop and reach out for help:

"Hello," a shaky voice answered.

"Ma?"

I told my mom where I was and she said she'd come right away.

At the end of Jacquelin's novel, Cary talks to her mother about why she ran away, and her mother says that *"she would do what she could to change things."*

On my next visit to see my father at his nursing home I told him about the dusty boxes in the largest closet in his basement.

"Dad, did you know Jacquelin wrote two novels?"

"Yeah, I think so." He didn't sound too sure.

"Do you want me to bring them here so we can read them together?"

"No."

He was still angry at Jacquelin for taking her life.

When I first found the novels, I was not ready to read them either. In fact, I didn't feel ready until I stumbled on them again when I was closer to finishing the first draft of this memoir, over four years after her death. Reflective-writing-time in my journals and planning Jacquelin's funeral had helped to get me ready.

***

From where I sat in my parents' kitchen I watched and listened to how thirteen-year-old Jacquelin spoke to her friend Arlene—not at all how twelve-year-old Jacquelin's protagonist Cary engaged with her friend Sara in the novel. Jacquelin's voice held familiar undertones of impatience, judgement, and irritation. Perhaps because my mother and I were there, Arlene only squirmed in silence. I sensed Arlene was wondering how to successfully navigate my sister's mood swing. When Arlene did speak, the more she placated, the more obtuse Jacquelin became. At one point Jacquelin got up to make herself a sandwich and just as she sat down to eat it, my mother spoke up.

"Jacquelin, aren't you going to offer Arlene something to eat?"

"She knows where the food is."

I held my tongue. My mother didn't.

"Jacquelin, you're being very rude."

"It's okay Mrs. Brewer," said Arlene, "I'm not hungry anyway."

"See," said Jacquelin.

Having pushed her chair away from the table, my mother opened the fridge. "Arlene, do you like a ham and cheese on brown?"

"Y-yes…but—"

I shifted in my seat. "Arlene, let my mom make you a sandwich."

Arlene and her brother lived two doors over from our west-end house and for one whole summer, when I was fifteen, it was my first good-paying childcare job.

I watched my mother at the counter. "Mom, Arlene likes lots of Mayonnaise."

"And mustard?" asked my mother.

"Yes please, that would be great."

I nodded and Jacquelin shrugged.

The scene was embarrassing, and I wasn't feeling proud of my sister's behaviour. But I did have an uncomfortable hunch. I intuited something unfathomable. Something had happened. There was a guardedness about Jacquelin. A vulnerability too. A wound. Something she wasn't talking about.

Jacquelin had been travelling by public transit back to our west-end neighbourhood to spend weekends with Arlene. On some of those weekends, she stayed at the family's trailer park. But for reasons beyond what I knew at the time, when the two girls were in their teens, their friendship got rocky. I had a hunch it had nothing to do with the long bus rides. Or unmade sandwiches.

After that embarrassing scene in my mother's kitchen, I had a private moment with Jacquelin.

"What's going on, Jacq?" I jumped to the chase, "Did something happen at the trailer?"

A secret. One Jacquelin stayed silent about until she told me many years later. I have a hunch her silence shaped what was to come.

***

In 1980 I had moved to St. Catharines to work at my dream job and, out of homesickness, I visited Toronto often. On one of those trips, I met a long-time friend in the mall close to our old high school. After lunch, she pointed to a young girl—thin and fully clad in black.

"Isn't that your sister?"

I barely recognized Jacquelin in tight-fitting jeans and a waist-length leather jacket with silver studs.

"Yes, it is."

"Did she just come up from the pool hall?"

My heart missed a beat.

"Looks like it—"

"Skipping classes?"

I studied my youngest sister. "Could be."

I chewed the side of my mouth and watched Jacquelin head towards a bench between two indoor trees reaching for the mall's skylight. The girls she stood bedside looked like her, skinny, heavily made-up, and clad in black. The tough look.

I wondered how my mother was not seeing this? Where the hell were my parents in this?

"They must be her new friends," I muttered. "Karen and Sophie. Maybe they're on a spare."

"You think so?"

I wasn't in the mood for aspersions about my truant sister. With all of the distractions of my pending divorce at the time, leaving one job and starting another in a different region, how long was it since I'd seen her? She had lost weight and I had no idea she was into white-powder face makeup and painting her eyes black. Seeing my sister through someone else's gaze was difficult. It would have been easier if I'd been alone. I guarded against my interpretation of my friend's tone.

Jacquelin saw me.

"Hi Jacq."

"Hi." She sounded meek.

"You doing okay?"

"Yep." She sounded defiant. Or unsure? Was she rattled by my "older sister and wannabe mother" presence?

"Good." I looked into her eyes. "Talk to you later?"

"Yeah, probably." She sounded indifferent. Or was she just acting cool in front of her new friends, trying to save face and resentful for being caught?

As I walked away, I sensed her icy blue eyes on my back. I suspected she felt cursed by bad luck.

I told my friend I didn't want to leap to conclusions. After all, with the high school just two blocks away, she could have been on a break between classes. But a pool hall? I'd never set foot in one. How judgmental was I? Was this me wavering between older sister and wannabe mother? Was I forgetting teen Jacquelin resided in the experiential part of her life?

"You're not going to stay and talk to her?"

"No."

"Are you going to tell your parents?"

"Probably not." If my mother's old practice of grounding came to the surface, I knew Jacquelin would be confined for at least a week. Personally, I never found that helpful.

"Don't you think they have a right to know?"

We kept walking while I mulled over her question.

"I think I'll leave that up to her."

I didn't tell my parents about Jacquelin coming out of the pool hall during school hours.

***

From my mother I heard about a neighbourhood party that got out of hand. Jacquelin was there. Trusting parents had gone to Florida for a hard-earned vacation and left two teenage daughters in charge of the family home. Teenagers came from everywhere, and the situation was any parent's nightmare. It sounded like the kids were terrified too. Jacquelin told me that she and Sophie fled the scary situation.

I never heard if anyone got hurt, but the damage to the house due to flooding and violent wreckage destroyed a beautifully appointed home. As teenage rage erupted, neighbours contacted the girls' parents and the police were called to the scene. Karen's firefighter father nor her mother could have prepared for such a horrific scene.

After the dismantling of that family's home, Karen was the first to fade away from the friendship of three.

There was no question Jacquelin's early drug and alcohol use was bringing her into harm's way. My alarmed and disappointed parents were in a panic. To help my sister, her friends, and two sets of distraught parents, I offered to facilitate the same kind of session I did with my students in the Basic Job Readiness Training program. The parents of Jacquelin's friend, Sophie, were also befuddled by their daughter's behaviour, and offered their home for our two sessions. Dates were set and everyone but Karen and her family attended. I lugged in a flip-chart stand and a film projector borrowed from the college. We watched a current film on adolescent drug and alcohol abuse. Sharing and discussion followed. In the beginning the girls were sullen and quiet and with some urging they did participate. There was no room for shame in the discussion. I think I was successful at normalizing the girls' experimentation, but still cautioned them about the harm of illicit drug use. The film showed how things could go and it appeared to me that neither Jacquelin or Sophie had considered the negative consequences.

When I think back about the intervention now, it was fortunate how well it worked out. It felt good to be there, and I knew both sets of parents, who had been feeling way out of their league, were grateful for the support.

Jacquelin and I talked about it later, and I sensed her relief. The following Christmas, Jacquelin bought me a generous gift. I think that was her unspoken way of saying thank you.

Thinking back, I remember when I had difficulty threading the film. My father stood up to help, but when the projector righted itself, I noted the grin of satisfaction on his face.

To my mother, he smiled and said, "She knows what she's doing."

My dad, who built physical structures and repaired almost anything that had moving parts, liked when he could help his daughters do the same. But Jacquelin didn't have the kind of problem my dad knew how to fix. I'm not sure they understood that I had placed my professional self into one of our family's struggles.

***

To get help for her troubled daughter, my mother made an appointment with the high school principal. Melody, who was still living at home, went with her. My mother didn't drive, so perhaps Mel went along for that reason. Or maybe it was about moral support, or both. Later that evening, Mel called to give me a blow-by-blow description of how things went.

"Mr. Campbell," my mother said, "I think it's disgusting how all these young people are lying around out there on school property." According to Melody, my mother's disparaging remarks caught the principal off guard and his retort came out sounding defensive.

"What is it that you want talk to me about, Mrs. Brewer?"

"I came to talk to you about my daughter. But now that I see that mess out here," she said, gesturing to the school's lawn on the other side of the large window. When I attended that school in 1974, I wasn't a part of the crowd that sprawled on the school lawn or cuddled in the back seats of parents' vehicles in the parking lot.

"I don't want this environment for my daughter. She's already in enough trouble, and I don't think staying at this school is going to help her. *That*—out there," she said, still pointing, "is a breeding ground for trouble."

According to Melody, the principal had no response. On the way out of the building, my mother said, "He was absolutely useless."

"Mom, what were you expecting?"

"A hell of a lot more than what we got. I tell you Melody, this place is a cesspool."

"Mom, Bev and I both graduated from here. It's not a bad school."

"Oh yeah? Well, I'm not convinced."

Back in my parents' kitchen, Jacquelin announced that she didn't want to go to school.

"I'm quitting."

For my mother, the image of the high school was fresh. So was her distaste for the principal, Mr. Campbell.

"Are you sure that's what you want?"

"Yep."

"Okay then. Quit."

When Melody repeated this story to me, it seemed my mother had given up. I was appalled. But what happened the next morning revealed that Mom had a plan.

After my father left for work, she knocked on Jacquelin's bedroom door. When she opened it, Jacquelin was still asleep.

"Jacquelin," she called.

"Yeah."

"Time to get up."

"Why? I'm not going to school—"

"Yes, I know that. But you have work to do."

When Jacquelin raised her head, she saw what my mother was holding—a paint brush in one hand and a gallon of paint in the other.

"What's that for?"

"It's for you. You've got work to do…Just because you're not going to school, don't think you're going to lie around all day. Oh no, if you stay home, you'll be working."

Jacquelin groaned.

"So, get up. I want you to paint the garage door."

According to Mel, Jacquelin did as my mother told her and, the next day, she went back to school. But not to the same school she'd been attending. My mother had decided her daughter's previous school had let her down. And that's why she walked—or according to Jacquelin, marched—her daughter to another school.

Jacquelin's dramatic makeup—white skin, dark eyes and black lips—eventually softened. And as she regained a healthy weight, tight-fitting jeans and leather jackets were pushed to the back of the closet.

It was a midterm entry, and Jacquelin scraped by to get her secondary school diploma.

Following in Mel's footsteps, she worked part-time at a small local pharmacy while she was a student. This was what my mother wanted.

"Keep Jacquelin busy."

Twenty-one
Friendship in the Midst of Trees

Fall 1996

Jacquelin and I were both enthusiastic about exercise and staying in shape. She lifted weights in the workout room in her basement. I preferred classes where I could get instruction from a fitness expert.

We both valued being outdoors. We ran or walked together in sync. Running along the cottage road on summer weekends was a favourite. Familiar with each curve, gully, and plateau of the road, we weren't only connected with one another but with the terrain.

To avoid the hot sun, we headed out before a full cottage breakfast. If it wasn't too hot, our dogs, her Bella and my chocolate lab, Major, came along. In the city—fall, winter and spring—we ran on quiet city streets and through ravines, parks, and cemeteries. I smile at the memory of being with Jacquelin in Mount Pleasant Cemetery when a small fox scampered among the tombstones behind us. Each time we caught sight of the critter, it stopped to peek at us from behind a gravestone.

"We're being stalked," I said.

"He's creepy," she said, assuming the fox was male.

"He's curious."

"Do you know that for sure or are you just making that up?"

"It's a feeling I have."

"Oh, that's good. I feel way better now."

I chuckled.

We wore proper shoes and clothes that evaporated sweat quickly. Being an avid water-drinker, Jacquelin was a good influence, insisting we start out with filled water bottles. Our arrangements for a run were planned ahead, but a walk could spill out of a spur-of-the-moment phone call. The calls were usually quick.

"Hi. What's up?"

"Not much. How's it going?"

"Good. You?"

"Pretty good."

"I thought about going for a walk…"

Her words were tentative, as if she ready to hear me say "no." I don't think I ever did.

"Alright. Wanna come here?"

She did.

Jacquelin's house was a fifteen-minute drive away. She didn't like to leave her dog Bella alone, so when I'd see both of them at the front door, I was never surprised.

"Is Bella running with us?" I asked.

"No, she can keep Major company."

"Sounds good."

We ran deep into a trail neither of us had taken before. The weather turned and we got drenched in the rain.

"Do you know where we are?"

"No, not really. But we're not lost."

"Humph."

"But I know one thing for sure…"

"What?"

"I've wrecked a new pair of running shoes. Look at my feet."

"Yeah, they're toast."

I suggested we get out of the ravine without backtracking. I surveyed the hillside.

"Keen on a hill climb?"

I took the lead. It was really slippery. Halfway up, I asked, "You doing okay?"

"Yeah. You?"

"Yep. Whose brilliant idea was this anyway?"

Laughing at ourselves, we traversed the slope diagonally, expressing thanks to tree roots and hardy shrubs sturdy enough to grab and hold our weight. With a lot of sliding, there was a bit of cursing too. But most of all, we laughed.

I had a tumble that day. I fell onto my back and slid in the mud three or four feet down the hill into a small bush engulfed in dried-out oak leaves.

"Are you okay?"

It was a soft landing.

Exploring ravines with Jacquelin reminded me of my childhood. There was a forested ravine at the end of our west-end street and it was like a playground for my friend, Rose, and me. We followed well-worn paths among the mature trees growing on the hillside not far from Black Creek, a tributary of the Humber River. At the top of the valley, we would walk the railway tracks that would take us as far as Union Station., but we never went that far.

The wood's rooty pathways took me further away from my mother's watchfulness. I felt like an explorer. Even on a bright day, foliage from the gnarly old trees kept out the light. The trees weren't as ancient as the ones in British Columbia, but the forest still had a mystical feel to it. I liked how it smelled—moist and fresh—and the unpredictability of what we might find at each twist in the path made it more fun.

In the bush, I was free.

I told Jacquelin about a time when I was around ten or eleven years old.

"Rose and I ended up behind the stockyards over on Keele Street. We got carried away following a cat who led us to a body."

Jacquelin rolled her eyes. "You followed a cat and found a body?"

"The cat just showed up out of nowhere on the railway tracks and we hoped she was taking us to her litter. Instead, we found a man. He looked more dead than asleep and it scared the hell out of us and we ran home along the railway tracks to tell our parents. The police were called."

"Was he dead?"

"No. The cop said he was likely sleeping off a bender and he wasn't too happy about us finding him. According to Mom, the cop said it would be a lot of paper work for nothing." When I was young, I hadn't absorbed his comment as a sad statement about help for alcoholism.

The ravine set the stage for filling Jacquelin in about our parents during my childhood. Anyone else who knew me, was aware of how strict our parents had been with me. But Jacquelin didn't. They were almost different people with her.

"At fifteen or sixteen, I still had to be in before the street lights turned on. Before I could go to a party, Mom interviewed other people's mothers. I wasn't allowed to go into cars, and motorcycles were a no-no. Friends and cousins felt sorry for me."

"I'm beginning to feel sorry for you too—"

"Other kids' parents thought Mom was too hard on me. Luckily, she was easier at the cottage. But in the city, she watched me like a hawk. That's likely why I loved disappearing into the bush so much."

"Probably. You still like the bush."

"Yeah, and if I was nowhere in sight, Mom gave Dad the job of calling me for dinner. He'd think nothing of bellowing my name from the front veranda. 'BEVERLEY!...BEV-ER-LEEEY...'"

"Oh my God, I'd hate that...that would be so embarrassing."

"It was." I chuckled. "Hearing my name yelled onto the street was humiliating. But it worked because I'd run like a deer and get my ass home."

"Holy crap. I'm glad they never did that to me."

"But hey...I remember you at fifteen or sixteen. You had a friend over to the cottage, and the two of you went to a party and stayed out really late."

"Yeah—"

"Mom and Dad got in the car and went looking—"

"It was a party over on Redwing."

"According to Mom, she stayed in the car while Dad traversed down the hill in the dark toward the music. It's cliffy over there and apparently Dad fell down over the rocks."

"I heard." She grunted unsympathetically.

"Good thing he didn't hurt himself."

"He was fine."

"Did you get grounded?" I asked.

"I don't remember. I think they just nagged a lot."

I wasn't there, but I could imagine. Later when I found the novel she wrote, *Running Away*, there were my parents—nagging.

"For sure they were harder on you," she said, "harder on you than they were on me or Mel."

"Yeah. Sometimes I felt stifled. "

"Not surprised…It sounds awful."

In the ravine with Jacquelin there was no resistance. It felt good to share a piece of my life story with her. Our time together felt close and warm. It felt like friendship.

Twenty-two
Wine for Breakfast

May 2010

On the morning of my fifty-fifth birthday, Jacquelin called.

"Happy Birthday." She sounded excited about giving me my gift and invited me over for coffee.

"That would be nice, thank you. I have a class at 11:35," I said. "I could come by around nine-thirty."

"Great," she said. "Umm...would you happen to have a bottle of wine you could bring over?"

I said nothing about the oddity of her request. "Y-yeah sure, I can do that."

When I got to her house, a man was in her living room.

"Bev, this is Brad, Carl's friend."

Since Carl was now the very recent ex-fiancé, I was surprised to see a friend of his on the floor wedged between the plush couch and the square coffee table my dad had refinished. Brad's long legs extended beyond the table.

Jacquelin was scantily dressed and Brad looked right at home.

"Hello." He had a warm smile. "Nice to meet you." He was polite. "Jacquelin is helping me with my resume."

Hmmm...rebound, I thought. I found myself feeling sorry for Brad.

Before Jacquelin became unwell, she kept her house relatively neat. I remembered a time when a baby-gate blocked Bella, her beloved hypo-allergenic Portuguese water dog, from living-room access. When anyone with a dog visited, Jacquelin rolled up the Persian carpet, a house-warming gift from my parents. No one questioned Jacquelin's house pride, especially about the living-room. Her black and white photography hung on the walls. So did more of her own creations, including large canvas paintings done in the style of the Group of Seven.

Paper work never extended into Jacquelin's living room, she reserved that for her upstairs office. That's why Brad's laptop on her coffee table looked out of place. So did the loose papers, books, over-filled ashtrays, and a pair of melted-down tapers. Red wax had melted onto the table's blond oak and the cigarette burn stood out. At one time, those tables were kept in top-notch condition. The only normal thing about Jacquelin's house was the strong scent of coffee. She always had a pot of brewed expresso on hand.

Brad and I made idle chat until he elaborated on his career aspirations. I stood in the doorway and Jacquelin gave me the gift bag and took the wine from my hand.

She glanced at the label. "Nice. Thanks."

She added the bottle to a case of wine sitting inside the entrance of the living room. Bewildered, I wondered why she'd asked me to bring wine when she already had several bottles. Perhaps she was worried about running out of booze.

She reached for a different bottle. I noticed she didn't take a second to read the label. In the kitchen she retrieved a corkscrew.

I scrutinized from the doorway, and not being able to help myself, said, "Jacquelin, you're not opening that now, are you?"

She appeared to think about my question. "No, I guess not."

I looked at Brad and may have detected relief.

She left the unopened wine on the counter, and I, acting as if nothing was askew, dug into the gift bag.

"Jacq, this is lovely. I need one of these."

It was a bathing-suit cover, soft-white and feminine.

"Yeah, I thought you might like it." Jacquelin had once told me she made a point to choose presents she would also like for herself. At the time, I thought the cover, though lovely, was more to her taste than mine.

I thanked and hugged her—never did get a cup of coffee—and said goodbye to the man who was getting help with his resume. I drove north on Victoria Park Avenue and replayed the scene in my head. I detected Brad's admiration for my sister was mixed was concern. He was smitten, came across as genuine, and I thought he might be the kind of man who would be good for my sister. That is, if she were willing. I wondered if he was wild enough. No, he wasn't, I could tell. I didn't think she was ready to settle into a space with saneness, predictability, and all that comes with love—sacrifice, reciprocity, honesty. I thought Brad should know better; after all, couldn't he see she was grieving a loss, an engagement that had gone south? Part of me felt sorry for him. As Carl's friend, he must have known about the turbulence in their short-lived relationship. Had he not considered rebound or seduction?

Not long after my birthday, I heard that Brad was no longer in her life. Then a little while afterwards, I was introduced to one of the men Jacquelin met on a dating website. The second time I met him was in Jacquelin's messy kitchen, and he told me about his strong feelings about my sister. He talked to me about how smart she was and her potential. He liked her sense of humour and mentioned her good looks. He really wanted to take care of her, he said. The man also called my dad and said the same. He was trying to help her drink less, he said, and then he wasn't in her life much longer either.

Twenty-three
Pass over the Phone

April 2011

My mother's complexion turned grey a few seconds after she answered the phone.

"Oh…oh…m-my oldest daughter is here. Why don't I let you talk to her."

As she passed me the phone her voice cracked. "H-here…it's Jacquelin's neighbour."

"Hi June, it's Bev. What's going on?"

"Jacquelin's in trouble. I can't just watch this happen. I did that with the man on the other side of me and I've never forgiven myself. My daughter-in-law who works at CAMH told me the family has to know what's going on. So now, I'm phoning."

"She's right…Th-thanks for calling…What is going on? Is…is Jacquelin okay?"

"No, she isn't. I just came from shooing away neighbours who were gawking through the living room window. One of them thought she was dead…An ambulance was called."

The skin on my face tingled and my heart missed a beat.

"What hospital?"

My parents gaped at me in silence.

"No, no…They didn't take her," said June. "They came, went inside, and left again."

"She's still at her house?"

"Yes, she is still in the house."

I nodded my head so my parents would know June's answer. I did my best to console my mother with my eyes.

"Look, this has been going on for a while," June said. "I should have called earlier—"

"It's so good you're calling now—"

"And there's lots of people coming and going—"

"Oh..." My stomach clenched. The picture in my mind got darker. I took a deep breath. "Men?"

She breathed deeply too. "Y...yes." Her voice was low.

My mother's eyes said she was either afraid or angry.

Mom asked, "Who is there now?"

Her question was loud enough, June heard it too. From how June cleared her throat I could tell she didn't like the question. I regretted the shift in her tone of voice.

"No, no...I'm not doing that..." she snapped.

"June, I totally understand—"

"Jacquelin is my friend." Still snappy.

"Yes, I know." I knew about the friendship and appreciated it.

"I'm not going to be tracking her—"

I felt light-headed and down. "I understand...You just wanted us to know."

"Yes. I'll never forget how lovely Jacquelin was with my late husband. He had Alzheimer's and he wandered, and she always helped me."

I had heard about June's worries. Jacquelin and she weren't just neighbours, they were good friends who watched out for one another. June taught Jacquelin about gardening and growing a perfect lawn. Jacquelin had a wise friend in June.

Minutes after the call ended, my parents were in their van on the way over to Jacquelin's. I followed in my car. It was a five-minute drive. When we turned onto the dead-end street, there was no sign of neighbours.

On the phone, June had said, "I always felt relieved whenever I saw your father's blue van pull into her driveway."

If she was watching from her window, I imagined her relief. Or guilt.

I watched the chubby orange cat saunter across the road. Often, he'd be curled up on one of the wicker chairs on Jacquelin's veranda.

My dad used his key. Without a knock we walked into the kitchen. Jacquelin, skeletal, sat at her glass-top café table smoking a cigarette. Wearing a worn pair of track pants, with legs tucked into chest, and arms wrapped around knees.

"What are you three doing here?" She sounded belligerent.

I collected chairs for everyone. My mother spoke first.

"The woman next door called us."

I gulped. I had hoped for a different approach.

"Who cares about them?" said Jacquelin. From her tone, I could tell she didn't "give a shit" about the neighbours.

"Jacquelin," I said, "It was June who called us. She's worried about you."

She softened. "Yeah well, she's a good person."

"Yes, she is, and so are you. You're in trouble right now. Let us help you—"

"You're no fucking angel."

I stood my ground. "You're right about that. But now, let's talk about getting you some help."

My mother got up from the chair. "I can't take this!"

I don't know if it was how Jacquelin annunciated the F-word or what my mother feared would come out of Jacquelin's mouth next, but she rushed to the door. I suspected the panic in her voice was driven by fear. Jacquelin appeared to take no notice of my mother's abrupt exit. Dad and I said nothing, nor tried to stop her.

My sister's blotchy skin and bloated face spoke to how unhealthy she'd become. Train wreck came to mind. Her house didn't look so good either. It smelled stale and the recycling box in the corner overflowed with take-out containers. The sink overflowed with plates and blackened pans. An untouched pizza sat on the counter.

My father was clear, "You're coming home with us. You can't stay here alone."

He was echoing my thoughts. She couldn't be trusted not to go to a darker place. I knew what he wanted: to guard her from alcohol and from the strangers she was letting into her house.

When Jacquelin and her dog Bella finally climbed into the back seat of my dad's van, my mother was smoking in the front seat. I looked into her eyes, and she turned away. She wasn't just angry at Jacquelin. She was angry at everyone.

I kept it simple, "Mom, I'll call you later."

"Yeah. Yeah."

She wasn't listening.

***

At home with Jack, I unveiled the details of Jacquelin's situation and the impact I feared it would have on my aging parents.

"She's staying with them," I said. "They're in over their heads with this one."

"Yep, and she'll walk all over them," he said. "They shouldn't be rescuing her."

"I know…They're just doing their best," I said.

He'd come across as angry. So defensively, I added, "Jack, they can't *not* do anything. I agree, it's not where she should be. I think she'd be better off here."

He didn't respond.

"She should be in rehab," I added, trying to say the right thing. I hated being in-between Jack and my sister. "But until she…admits—"

"Yep. But she won't likely go. She's not sick enough. The landings have been soft. You and your parents keep rescuing her…She hasn't hit real bottom yet."

I wondered how he thought he was so sure. I wasn't nuts about his directness either. At the same time, how she looked and spoke to us wasn't how I knew her. Her beloved house, the one she worked so hard to pay for and decorate in her own style, was in shambles. So was her life. Imagining a deeper bottom for my sister intensified my fright.

After talking a lot more with Jack—which helped me think straight—I called my parents.

"Hi Mom. Jack and I are coming over to take Jacquelin to an AA meeting."

"She's not feeling very good," she said.

The phone was on speaker and Jack got involved, "Jackie, it's the best time for her to go to a meeting…before she starts feeling better."

My mother usually listened to Jack. "Okay, whatever you think."

Did Jacquelin agree to go? As wobbly and sick as she was, yes, she did.

One hour later in the church's basement, Jacquelin and I were the only women in the room. I'd wished for a different ratio. Had a wise woman with seasoned sobriety come along, I would have moved aside. I didn't want to be the only woman holding her up.

Did Jacquelin continue to attend? From what I heard, she went more often than I knew about—which gave me solace—but I also heard she didn't always stay. One person said she appeared disengaged. I had to keep telling myself it was Jacquelin's journey to live. But I wasn't doing so well at staying on track.

She might have lasted a couple of nights at my parents. I got it—I wouldn't have wanted to be back in my parents' house either. When she stayed with us, it was the same. She'd feel better and leave. People told me alcoholics have short memories and I figured that was just a cute way of saying the person didn't want to stop drinking. It was hard to watch her go back to a dark messy house while she was so unchanged.

Over the phone, on May 6th 2011, my mother told me Jacquelin had been picked up for drunk driving. I couldn't have felt any more sorrow. I was also mad as hell.

I sighed heavily into the receiver. "How could she do something so stupid? And where the hell was she going that she had to drive drunk?"

Standing on my back deck with the cellphone pressed into my ear, I pictured my parents across from one another in their kitchen. They'd put their phone on speaker.

My father, answered my question, "She was heading westbound on the Gardiner Expressway. They picked her up at York Street."

That suggested she was going to Mississauga. The new fella, several years younger than her— the one I referred to as on-and-off-boyfriend or boy-toy. He lived in his parents' basement in what Jacquelin described as a wealthy neighbourhood.

Everyone in the family was flabbergasted when they heard about the impaired driving charge. Feelings of disbelief, disillusionment, and sorrow—with anger and fear in the mix—came close to what I had only begun to feel about my sister's life.

Someone said, "It could happen to anyone. It doesn't take much to blow over."

"She could have killed someone," Mom moaned. Still on speaker phone, she told me to go and get her.

"No, I don't think she should," snapped my father. He sounded livid. "Let Jacquelin stew in there for a while. Maybe it will teach her a lesson."

I wrestled with my inner-thoughts. What's better? Tough love or rescuing?

Jacquelin must have given the lawyer my number because just after three o'clock, I got a call.

"Court closes at five. You don't want to leave your sister in a cell over the weekend. She's unwell and doesn't belong here." I heard concern and empathy in his voice. "She needs help with her problem," he said. "If she stays in here, she'll get eaten alive."

What did he mean by "unwell?" It was something I still hadn't come to terms with. While I put that thought on hold, my mind went to my first job after university at the Observation and Detention Centre on Jarvis Street. I worked three shifts, including the nasty overnight from eleven to seven o'clock in the morning. Some of the young offenders called us workers "turnkeys," and when my supervisor made the grave mistake of telling a couple of them that I was married to a police officer, I became known as "Pig Lover."

Later, while still thinking academically about a career path in Corrections, I interviewed at the Vanier Prison for Women where I couldn't convince the warden or her officer, I was right for the job.

"You'll get eaten alive in here," said the warden not mincing her words.

When I sat beside the lawyer on an oak bench inside the courthouse, with the intention of bailing Jacquelin out, I recall my surprise when he opened his black leather briefcase. He took out the small bank machine.

"I pay right here and now?" I was expecting an invoice.

Patient and gentle, he nodded. No doubt he could tell I'd never done this before and that for me, everything was happening quickly. (In my first job at the detention centre, I accompanied kids to court but I had no experience with what went on in the hallway outside the courtroom.)

"How much is it?" I asked.

"One-thousand dollars."

I pulled out my credit card.

"We don't take credit," he said.

Surprised again, "Oh—"

"Cash or debit."

I gave him my debit card.

He flipped through papers, pointing to where I needed to put my signature, while sharing his thoughts.

"It's hard for me to understand alcohol abuse. I'm Muslim. I don't drink alcohol."

I listened.

"Your sister will have a criminal record now. She's made her life harder."

There was no denying her choices had caught up with her. I had wanted her life to get easier. That's why I'd been hovering and plotting a direction on her behalf.

Jacquelin in handcuffs was tormenting. She looked horrendous: slumped shoulders, half-ponytailed hair, and a pale face streaked with yesterday's mascara. Inside the box, cuffs were removed from her boney wrists.

Her panicked eyes searched the courtroom until she found me.

"I'm sorry," she mouthed.

Jacquelin would have known that someone from the family would come to her rescue. Still, I saw shame and shame could eat the guilty alive. Her vulnerability stabbed at my stomach and caused my heart to race.

With fingertips together at my mouth and my eyes locking into hers, I offered a slow nod.

Jacquelin stood before the judge, in front of a courtroom of people who heard the officer read out his report. When the officer finished, the judge made disparaging remarks about Jacquelin's recklessness—open liquor in the car—and her outright lack of regard for others and for the law. He sounded flummoxed by how much alcohol was in her blood.

"I've seen men four times your size die of lower levels…"

My first experience of a judge presiding over an impaired driving charge was during a student field trip to the courts in Toronto's Old City Hall. I have a vivid picture of the accused, a forty-year-old woman. Through sobs she told the judge about her mistake to drink and drive after she'd heard about her mother's cancer diagnosis. Unmoved, the judge countered her story with one of his own. He talked about a child whose life had been cut short because he'd been hit by a car driven by a drunk driver. I recall the breathlessness among my students who drank and drove.

I took the stand on the day Jacquelin was in court. The judge described the details about bail and he asked if I had enough money in the bank.

"Yes, Your Honour." Since I'd already used my debit card, the fee was out of my account.

Jacquelin's weepy blue eyes were on me as the judge reviewed the terms for her release to my care: no alcohol, a curfew, no operating a motor vehicle or riding in the front seat of one, no going anywhere without the full consent of the insurer (me), and making sure she'd show up for her next court date. She was going to be staying with me, so I told him I could handle all of that.

The lawyer was dead-on about the charge being life-changing. And not only for her. I was already engulfed in the lives of two people I loved deeply. I was walking alongside Jack in his battle with fourth-stage lung cancer. I'd been watchful over my dad's grief and his compromised health and dissolving independence. Jack and my dad were open to my help and even if they forgot to say, their immense appreciation sustained me.

I thought about some of my students who survived the hardships of addiction. Their grueling stories of living on the edges enriched my imagination. Pete comes to mind. He was a student in the Basic Job Readiness Training program. Pete had a previous heroin habit. I was convinced the twelve-week Basic Job Readiness Training program, with academic upgrading, job search, and life skills breathed a second chance into his life. I wasn't the only person to have a soft spot for him; everyone liked him. Similar to Jacquelin, he was lovable, except for the times when he consumed large amounts of fresh garlic in an attempt to ward off his drug cravings.

During one of our counselling sessions, his physical disclosure shocked me when he rolled up his sleeve to show me fresh needle marks.

"I could lie to you, but I'm not going to," he said.

Active drug use was not aligned with the program's goals and therefore not tolerated. I stayed quiet about policy. The purpose of our program was to help people find and keep employment, and illicit drug use or alcoholic drinking was not part of the equation.

"You've been doing so well. What happened?"

On the weekend, he'd met a girl who used heroin.

"Are you planning on using again?"

He looked away. Shame, I thought. "I'm so sorry. I'm not going to use again."

Good answer, I thought. I told him I had to share his disclosure with my colleagues, and he understood.

Pete graduated from our program, but I don't think he found work. Nor did he enroll in further training or education. In spite of his gregarious nature and how he could make others laugh, he had no real friends. No family. Months later, when I was working in another department at the college, my colleague Ann phoned to tell me Pete had died. He died in the front seat of his much-loved Dodge sedan parked in the lot outside the campus where I suspected he felt at home. His life ended with heroin.

There are few students in my teaching lifetime who haven't taught me something. It was part of the job that kept me feeling alive and satisfied. What Pete's too-short life showed me was the destructive power of loneliness and isolation. I saw the same play out in my sister's life. From Pete's story in the counselling session, I heard it took seconds to go back to heroin. I have come to understand the cycle of shame in an addict's life. When Pete told me about his relapse, his eyes left my face and he hung his head. Shame? I had the impression he wanted to hide. The time I saw Jacquelin stand before the judge in the courtroom, I recognized the same burdened emotion. Excruciating to witness it in a person you love.

***

Jacquelin had attempted to dance on the skinny edges of darkness. Not for a minute did I ever think she was prepared. She wasn't as equipped as some of my students. I never told her about Pete, but I tried to convey stories about students who acquired new life skills and survived.

Again, the curt, "I'm not like your students, Beverley."

Jacquelin didn't know how my imagination kicked into over-drive and how I easily pictured someone shoving a needle into her arm. My rawest fear. I was afraid she'd come across an unsavory dance partner who would sniff out vulnerability and do her harm.

Twenty-four
A Painful Cottage Visit

July 2015

In her darkest times, Jacquelin started to feel like a stranger. One time I convinced her to come to the cottage. I thought getting away from the city and her boyfriend would be good for her. She used to embrace the cottage as a sanctuary and a place to catch her breath. I wanted Jacquelin to be well so we could rekindle our past relationship. I anticipated a walk on the cottage road, taking the canoe she had painted red out for a paddle around the island, and then hanging out on the dock. I told her I missed doing those things with her and I would love to do them again.

She didn't look at me. "I don't know if it can ever be like that again, Bev."

I heard an ending.

Soon after we arrived, I got the sense she didn't want to be at the cottage. Too painful. On reflection, I was likely too enthusiastic and overly encouraging about the idea. At one point during the visit, I saw her behind the cabin, weeping.

"It's hard, eh Jacq."

At the cottage, remnants of an earlier life with my parents were, and still are, everywhere. Every nook, holds a trace of my mother's suggestions and my father's physical work. They cleared the land and built each structure—cottage and two cabins— from the ground up. I considered Jacquelin was grieving our mother's death and the absence of our father's capabilities, then at age eighty-six, I was grieving those losses too. She didn't talk to me about her tears. She didn't engage. She was like a fragile rock.

Later in the day Jack showed Jacquelin how to use the electric hammer. She seemed to enjoy the task and for a couple of moments I found my heart reaching for hope.

Her interest was short lived.

A friend of Jack's had dropped in for a visit, and, since he was heading back into the city, I asked him if he would give Jacquelin a lift back home. He claimed he was only going as far as Highway 7. I didn't believe him.

Jacquelin overheard my request. I dramatically rolled my eyes at her.

She shrugged, "Don't worry about it, Beverley," and walked away.

I did worry. I had felt certain cottage time would breathe life into her. It hadn't.

She'd had enough rejection. I worried she was on the verge of impending doom. What did I do? I owned it and I drove her home.

It was a quiet drive south.

Four hours later, I arrived back at the cottage, poured a cool drink, and returned to my book club read, *The Liar's Club*. Mary Carr wrote a story that would be difficult to disguise as anything else but deep suffering. For that reason, I put the book aside. My head was too full to take in any more suffering.

Outside on the deck I leaned over the railing to notice oak leaves I had raked into a pile with the notion of burning them in the barrel. I didn't feel up to the task. It was almost dusk. I needed my brain to shut down. A soft wind rustled through the trees and I decided I was up for a kayak. With each dip of the paddle, I propelled the craft into the golden sunset.

Twenty-five
Looking for Answers in the Literature

January 2021

I looked for books about grieving suicide loss. I went out of my way to read about other peoples' experiences of losing a loved one to mental illness. Memoirs on this subject reassured me that loving a sibling who took their own life was not neat and tidy. Death can be complicated enough, and suicide stories are messy and not easy to tell.

I put myself on a long library waitlist for Don Gillmor's *To the River: Losing My Brother* (2018).

Some aspects of the relationship with his brother resonated and I recognized Gillmor's quest for understanding about depression, and the pain his brother's journey brought to his family, friends, and himself, even though the two brothers were estranged from time to time.

In Miriam Toews's novel, *All My Puny Sorrows* (2014) the rapport between sisters Elf and Yoli mirrored how Jacquelin and I communicated. Raw emotions gurgled. Similar to how Toew's character Yoli observed Elf, I was acutely familiar with Jacquelin's mannerisms. I noticed mundane things like lip clenching, hair twirling and nail biting, followed by fake fingernails to camouflage the damage.

How many times did I see my sister's hands shake? How often did I sense she was in pain even when we weren't in the same house? When I called to check in, did Jacquelin hear tension? When we were face-to-face, did she recognize I was acting. My sister covered bloody cuticles and I masked my dread. That's how we danced. Who was the bigger burden? To alleviate my part in that cumbersome waltz, I told myself to keep breathing and not to forget to pray. When I tried to make things right, my imperfections scared me. It was a strain not to say too much. Mis-steps were everywhere.

In *My Puny Sorrows*, Elf was not secretive about wanting to end her life. Jacquelin never directly used words to say she wanted to die. Her actions, like binge drinking and too much time with Boy Toy, spoke to that. It wasn't until after she left us, that Jacquelin clearly stated what she wanted. In her final note, she wrote, "My life is done," and on another line, "I cannot face what is coming." With more clarity than she usual, she wrote, "I hadn't wanted to live for a long time. It is and has been for a long time absolutely pointless."

Instead of self-destruction, I was hoping she would get back on the path of self-reliance. I think that's what she yearned for too. But it must have been too hard. I had the sense she was attempting to claw her way back up. I suspected she was in wordless pain about previous life goals that felt beyond her reach.

As Jacquelin put it, her life was hell.

In an early therapy session with psychologist Dr. Denisoff, I scanned her shelf and caught a glimpse of a book I once owned: *The Unquiet Mind: a memoir* by Kay Redfield-Jamison (1995). It was one I had given away but never forgotten. On my way home after my session I made a detour and bought myself another copy. Redfield-Jamison was a psychiatrist who treated patients with manic depressive bipolar illness and she wrote narratively about living with the disease.

In my second read of *The Unquiet Mind*, I recalled some of the characteristics of Redfield-Jamison's illness showing up more visibly in Jacquelin after she was laid off from a much-loved job in her early forties.

I remember the story of when Jacquelin was summoned to her employer's central office. She was not expecting good news so she had asked Mel to go with her. I am not sure if Jacquelin was fired for incompetency or if she was another unlucky employee caught in a company-wide layoff. A few months earlier, she had taken a new position with more autonomy than she could handle. When Mel and I became privy to how Jacquelin was managing her time, we cautioned her about being at the gym during the workday. I knew her boss well. We had gone to school together.

"Jacq, she's tough," I cautioned. "She's a hard worker with high expectations of everyone else."

"Don't worry Beverley, I know what I'm doing."

After the meeting Mel described the despair on Jacquelin's face when she walked back into the lobby. Given the loss of a job she loved, Jacquelin's response was within reason. I knew what Jacquelin's job meant to her identity. It would be hard, but I thought my sister had the resolve to move on and find a new job.

First, she took some time to do chores around her house. She did practical things like installing eavestroughs that had the added feature of a leaf guard. To refresh her wardrobe, she shopped for clothes. After the layoff, many of her early decisions were practical. Then, she began to spend money in ways she hadn't before, like ordering more take-out than she could ever eat. She got verbose and racy.

It didn't take her long to get hired at a telecommunications firm in Waterloo. But she hadn't considered the toil of the daily commute. Everyone in the family talked to her about it. The intensive training was challenging, and the long drive back and forth broke into study time. Still, I thought she would find herself settling back into a healthy routine. Then when she rushed into buying a house with a man she hardly knew, I recognized she was not thinking straight.

Desperate to make sense of Jacquelin's struggle, I found it helpful to talk about Jamison-Redfield's personal narrative with Dr. Denisoff. From my descriptive interpretation of Jacquelin's life, Dr. Denisoff suspected my sister suffered from bipolar disorder. I'd heard that before. Dr. S, a psychiatrist who met with Jacquelin two or three times, had said the same thing. Perhaps that's why Jacquelin stopped seeing her.

Almost four years after her death, I turned to the Centre for Addiction and Mental Health website.

Bipolar disorder is a medical condition characterized by extreme mood swings that affect how people think, behave and function. (www.camh.ca)

I wanted to see if Jacquelin's mood changes aligned with the description for the manic phase of bipolar disorder. I found a list:
- exaggerated self-esteem or feelings of grandeur
- decreased need for sleep
- more talkative than usual
- easily distracted
- excessive energy for activities
- engaging in risky behaviour or exhibiting poor judgement.

The list fit.

In the early days of grieving Jacquelin's death, it was difficult not to question what she was thinking about in the few hours before she ended her life. I read Anna Mehler Paperny's memoir, *Hello I want to Die Please Fix Me* (2019). Paperny's thoughts about killing herself made me wonder if Jacquelin's mind also was flooded with compulsive obsessions. If so, how often, and did the thoughts come in unstoppable waves? At nighttime, did Jacquelin envision horrible accidents or homicides? Paperny did. Her suicide ideations, sometimes sexual fantasies, were vivid and disturbing. Did Jacquelin also suffer these uninvited notions?

After she died, I came across selfies of Jacquelin and Siron, her dog. Sometimes she was in her adored Audi. The photos were taken after plastic surgery and after the bruising on her face and neck was gone. Jacquelin, though beautiful, did not look happy. In an odd way, she appeared younger than her years. I don't mean to imply the plastic surgery worked. It was more about her appearing naïve, lost, and scared to death.

Did my sister have a scorching thirst to be pulled away like how Paperny described? I think so. The particular selfie that took my breath away was taken in the bedroom at my dad's house. With unkempt hair and sallow complexion, she looked tired, unwell, and deeply sad. And alone. The image screamed vulnerability. Taken only a few days before she died, in this image that bothered me the most, Jacquelin's eyes had no fight for life left.

Jane Pearson, head of Adult Preventive Intervention and Chair of the Suicide Research Consortium at the National Institute of Mental Health (NIMH), reminds us about the distinction between "survival" and "self-extinction." Survival is instinctive and self-extinction is not. On reflection, when I looked again at the selfie, and into my sister's eyes, I did not see any fight for life.

The closest Jacquelin got to talking about her desire to end her life was seconds before she banged the phone down hard in my ear. "If I kill myself, it's on your head."

What was she saying about me in relation to her life? Was she attempting to make me responsible for her behaviour even though she fought hard against me?

I told Jack what she said.

"No good deed goes unpunished."

I groaned at his hackneyed phrase.

I can't be sure what Jacquelin meant, but if it was blame, I did not take responsibility for her distress. Several days passed before we spoke, and she was calmer and less distraught. It was part of our dance. But that did not mean either of us were better. Carefully, gently and as cautiously as I knew how, I asked her if I should worry about our last conversation. She said "no."

I suspected Jacquelin knew that if she had spoken plainly about self-harm, I would have put myself in her way. Telling me she planned to kill herself would have given me cause to get her help, even if it was against her will. She was informed about the conditions necessary for involuntary commitment to a psychiatric facility.

Twenty-six
Tough Love is Harder Than It Sounds

June 2016

Fourteen months before my sister's death, when she directed her rage at my dad, there were clear indications Jacquelin was in psychological trouble. Her unpredictability was putting him at risk, and my father had reason to tell her to leave his house and change the locks.

The next day at around three o'clock in the morning, I jumped out of bed to answer the phone. My dad's voice shook.

"Jacquelin's here."

"I'll be right over."

I dressed, called the police, and drove across Eglinton. It was still dark and the city was quiet. I arrived before the police. As I pulled up, Jacquelin was crossing the lawn. She had come out the side door. She was wearing a black cape over her long coat.

So as not to wake anyone, I whispered, "Jacquelin, don't go. Let's talk about this."

Her arms flailed into the air, and as she walked down the sidewalk, she chanted, "I am free. I am free. I am free."

Flabbergasted, I chose not to chase after her. I watched until I couldn't see her. When I went into the house, I found my dad, dressed in track pants and a T-shirt, sitting in the dark.

I sat across from him and noticed marks on his fragile arm.

"Did she hurt you?"

He said she tried to grab the phone off him when he was speaking to me.

"Dad, I thought you had the locks changed. Wasn't the locksmith here?"

"Yes. But Jacquelin was here at the same time. She must have taken the copies from coffee table, because they aren't there."

"Great—"

"I knew she was in the house. I went downstairs—"

Hearing that my infirm dad had been on the basement stairs rattled my nerves.

"I looked in the furnace room," he said. "She was sitting cross-legged on the floor, grinning at me."

"Oh my God…What did you say to her?"

"I told her to get up and get out of there."

"Dad, if she'd just co-operate. Quit drinking. Get help."

Despite the police escort off the property and the warning that she could land herself in a cell, she had come back at three in the morning. That meant that my father had to call the locksmith again. He was determined, but so was she. She made a cut long enough in the screen to crawl through it. I noticed the gouges on the window frame, so I gathered shovels and anything else that could be used to smash glass. I hid them. There was a lump in my throat as I did it. It was weird to be defending my father against my sister. It was my preference to talk to her, but she was so full of rage and hate, she could not hear me.

A day or two later, two familiar police officers escorted Jacquelin to my dad's house so she could pick up her things. Jack and Dad were there too. She was in full performance mode, which made me angry and sad at the same time. It bothered me that she had enough energy to put on an act. At one point she appeared smug and I suspected she was afraid.

I felt caught between our vulnerable father, whom I suspected had not told me everything, and my sister. I didn't think my dad was any closer to understanding how to manage Jacquelin's manic phase than I was.

While the police looked on, my dad asked her to move her vehicle from the front of his garage door. I assumed she ignored him because her breathalyzer would have prevented the car from starting. Strange sounds would have gone off.

It broke our spirits to witness her departure. This is the first time we implemented "tough love," and frankly, I had no idea what to do with myself. It was horrible to watch her move her stuff without offering a helping hand. When I went to speak to her, one of the cops told me to be quiet. I felt chastised. At one point, Jacquelin became softer and compliant, and I wondered if the officers were trained to recognize feigned innocence. When my sister was aggrieved, it was easy to sympathize. It was difficult to know if she was playing us. Trust was at an all-time low.

She had called a cab-van, and, when she went outside to meet the driver, I ignored the officer's glare and joined her.

"Jacq, where are you staying tonight?"

"None of your business."

"What if there's an emergency?"

"What kind of emergency?"

"Dad."

After a pause, she told me.

"Okay. Thanks."

Back in the living room, I interrupted the conversation between Jack and my dad to tell them where she was going.

My father's complexion had gone grey. "We'll see how that goes."

Jack nodded, and I wondered how not to fall deeper into the abyss between the people I loved. So far it had been the kind of day where nothing felt right.

Jacquelin's long-time friends knew she was coming but I found out later that they did not expect a mound of luggage. She didn't stay long. In a short time, she lied to them about her drinking, and they told her to leave. They felt awful about it. From there Jacquelin and puppy Siron moved from one hotel to another. Later, she told me she kept getting kicked out of hotels because of her smoking.

***

On January 15, 2017, at 12:50 a.m., Jacquelin left me a message saying, "If I die it will be your fault—you are a cold bitch." One week later in a call to my dad, she said, "I have no family. I may as well slit my throat."

"Jacquelin, come home," he repeated.

Each time he was clear about taking steps to get help for her problem. She didn't want help. She said she was "on vacation." Jacquelin was on a run.

When we lost track of her for three or four days in a row, I called cab companies and hotels in an attempt to track her down. When I spoke to the police sergeant who had been at the house, I think he felt sorry for me and, after one of our chats, he agreed to file a Missing Person's Report. The police sergeant also said it would help if I acquired a Form 1.

"With a Form 1, the police can take her to a hospital for an assessment."

By seven-thirty the next morning I was sitting on an oak bench beside the Office of the Justice of the Peace. One hour later, she listened to my story.

"Getting a Form 1 is hard on everyone, including the family," she said.

"It's already hard," I said.

"Your sister will know you were the one who requested the form."

She's already pissed with me, I thought.

"When the police pick her up, they'll put her in cuffs. It's hard to see."

"Yes, I know. I'm already seen my sister in cuffs." And yes, it's awful.

I left with a Form 1 and called the sergeant to let him know.

"You did well," he said. "They're not easy to get."

Soon after the missing report went into the system, two Kitchener-Waterloo police officers found Jacquelin in a coffee shop. She had travelled by cab from Toronto to Kitchener-Waterloo. From the dispatcher at the cab company, I learned that she stiffed the cabbie for the fee. That did not sound like Jacquelin at all and it's a point that makes me think she must have been in full manic mode. I'm not sure how she got back to Toronto.

According to the police officer, Jacquelin had said to him, "Do I look like I'm missing?" At the close of our conversation, he added, "She's quite funny."

"Yes," I said. "She can be."

She charmed them.

He also said, "And, she can sure talk."

"Yes, that's true as well." When she's manic.

Several hours later, around four o'clock in the morning, I was awoken by the sharp sound of the phone. A psychiatrist from one of the hospitals in Kitchener-Waterloo was on the other end of the line.

I can't remember exactly how he said it, but he told me she wouldn't likely kill herself. My brain filled with relief.

When the psychiatrist and addictions nurse met with Jacquelin, did they diagnose her accurately? Having encountered over-tired physicians in hospital units, I wondered if the psychiatrist had been working a double shift? Then I reminded myself that my bright articulate sister could be an excellent actor.

"She's an alcoholic," he said.

Did he not think alcoholics kill themselves? I did not ask that at the time. It was early and who knows how much I missed in my own state of stress. Later, I remembered three alcoholics who died by suicide in the last five years.

On the other hand, I also know many more alcoholics who are living fulsome lives in their recovery. That's what I wanted for Jacquelin. Therefore, in some small way, the psychiatrist gave me hope because I know there can be life after addiction. However, when he said, "Your sister needs treatment, and if she goes, I doubt she'll stay," my jaw tightened.

"Calls like this are the hardest ones for me to make." His was kind and honest.

"Yes. I can imagine."

Following more comforting words, he told me they were releasing her. The Form 1 was short-lived, null and void, and my sister was no longer considered a "missing person." She was found. No, not really.

Jacquelin's GP, Dr. K, had warned me that a Form 1 was not an effective intervention. Later I wondered if my panicked yearning to know her whereabouts, caused my sister more harm than good. The rollercoaster of emotions, including my second-guessing, intensified the fatigue and played havoc with my head. Would her having been "formed" show up on the background check for the job she wanted so badly? I turned to Google with my question.

In the search bar, I asked, "In Ontario, does a psychological assessment show up in a background check?"

Answer: "Police in Ontario won't be able to disclose mental health information and will only release non-conviction records in limited circumstances to potential employers and others in background checks under legislation introduced," (Google, Wednesday June 3, 2015.)

The day after Jacquelin had gone missing and was found again, Mel told me about their phone conversation.

"Jacquelin is really angry with you. And I quote, 'That bitch Beverley, reported me missing. Do you believe that? Do you know how embarrassing that is!'"

Mel's dramatic rendition of Jacquelin's words rang true.

"Jacquelin told me you wanted to lock her up," said Mel. "Is that true?"

"Clearly, that's how she sees it. What I want is for our sister to go into to rehab where she'll get some help for her problem."

I knew Mel and her husband were not strong proponents of recovery programs, and when Mel told me for the second time that she had advised Jacquelin to "just have a couple of drinks," I hit the roof.

"Mel, she's an alcoholic. A binge drinker. She can't just have one or two drinks! She needs help—"

"Well anyway, she's not going into rehab. She's going for more plastic surgery instead."

And she did. After one of her surgeries, Jacquelin signed into the Royal York Hotel and recovered there for three days. She hired a private nurse to stay with her. She told Mel cosmetic plastic surgery was something she had always wanted.

"Well, let's hope the surgery keeps her alive," I said.

Jacquelin was spending the income from the sale of her house. From receipts left behind, we know she spent at least forty-one thousand dollars on cosmetic plastic surgery.

Was the plastic surgery one more thing she thought she could do to make her feel worthwhile? My sister's physical features were always lovely, so the notion of her "under the knife," blew my mind. And given her alcoholism and the status of her mental health, my distrust of plastic surgeons deepened. I've since wondered what screening process a plastic surgeon has in place. Therefore, on August 1, 2022, at a point closer to completing this memoir, I went on Google. Embedded in the abstract of *Psychological screening measures for cosmetic plastic surgery patients: a systemic review*, I learned that scientifically sound and clinically useful tools to assess patients for their suitability for cosmetic surgery are still lacking. (Petra Wildgoose, Amie

Scott, Andrea L Pusic, Stefan Cano, Anne F. Klassen (@pubmed.ncbi.nfm.gov on August 1, 2022.)

Jacquelin's General Practitioner, Dr. K, knew about her depression. When I showed up in his office, he had been clear with me about confidentiality.

"I'm not here to ask. I'm here to tell," I said. "My sister has not been telling you the truth and I'm worried about her." He was the first professional I spoke to about obtaining a Form 1.

I remember his sorry eyes when he said, "It doesn't do any good."

Like the psychiatrist in Waterloo had, Dr. K had already spoken to her about attending sessions at CAMH, the Centre for Addiction and Mental Health.

"She didn't go," I said.

He shrugged his shoulders, and that told me I had hit another brick wall.

"She needs to stop drinking," he said.

"Yes, I know."

Jacquelin had showed him a letter claiming she had been going to AA meetings on a regular basis. Dr. K questioned why the writer hadn't included their full name.

"No one uses last names," Jacquelin told Dr. K.

She had coaxed a naive friend to write the letter. According to Jacquelin, Dr. K bought it. She thought she had outsmarted her doctor. I don't know whether Dr. K knew, but such letters are signed with a full name all the time.

Jacquelin behaved in ways that were not congruent with her earlier life. Stiffing a hard-working cab driver would have been out of the question. In fact, she was a generous tipper.

Dr. K prescribed at least two different antidepressants. I knew Jacquelin did not take the medication, because when I cleared out her room after she died, I came across bags of antidepressants, stapled shut. She had told Jack that she did not like how they made her feel. He encouraged her to give the meds some time. When she had called Dr. K, he said the same.

Dr. K was cross with her when he got the report that she had walked out of the hospital before treatment. Still, when I spoke to him again, he hadn't given up on her.

"Tell her to come and see me."

Dr. K had no idea of the loftiness of his suggestion. But what else could the doctor have done?

Deceit and desperation were embedded in her disease and as painful as it was to watch, I accepted that my sister was doing her best to keep afloat. Thinking this way helped me stay optimistic. Had I thought she was merely a self-serving party-girl, I am pretty certain I would have stepped away.

***

When she arrived back from Kitchener-Waterloo, Jacquelin called me from a hotel in Richmond Hill. I heard carousing in the background. She told me that one of the women, told her she didn't belong there.

"'Jacquelin, just go home.'"

"Jacq, she's given you good advice."

"Hmmm…"

"Call Dad. Work things out… Jacquelin, he wants you safe."

The next day, a long-time friend delivered Jacquelin to my dad's house.

No one wanted Jacquelin living on the street. That fear was why my dad said she could move back into the house for that final time. But unlike the first time she moved in, he insisted she stay in her old bedroom, now guestroom, on the main floor.

"And I'm not giving you a key to this house."

If she was going to come and go, he wanted to know about it. This was my father's way of keeping her safe.

My dad knew Jacquelin was getting calls from collection agencies. He agreed to cover her debts, and he was clear the money would come out of her inheritance. As they went through her stack of unopened envelopes, her life became an open slate. Jacquelin, the very private person, must have been horrified.

Invoices indicated that she had used an ambulance thirty-six times. I don't know what was going through her head when she made those calls. What kind of help did she want? Maybe she was out of booze and, with no valium at hand, was afraid of a seizure.

Jacquelin finally followed up on my encouragement to go back to Dr. K for a referral to the family therapy clinic.

I was direct: "Call the office right now and phone me back to let me know how it went."

She was compliant and let me manage her. Within minutes, she called me back to say she got an appointment. Aware of my control, I wondered if I should have been more directive earlier. Or was she just ready this time?

From the core of my soul, I said, "Jacquelin, what you just did is so important."

Her reaction was flat, and I told myself to "go slow," and let her take "one step at a time."

She liked the therapist and ended up working with her for almost two months. After Jacquelin took her life, Mel called the therapist to tell her the news. The therapist said that when she hadn't shown up for their session, she went to our father's house looking for Jacquelin. She would have seen the yellow-police tape across the door.

Twenty-seven
Labour Day Weekend

September 1 - 4, 2017

It always took my husband Jack a few days to recover from a chemo treatment, so he was content to retreat to the cottage to work on a crossword, watch his beloved Yankees, and keep the fire burning in the woodstove. I kayaked around the lake, walked the dogs, puttered in the garden, and chopped firewood. At the same time, my mind drifted to Jacquelin and my dad in Toronto.

After getting the call about my dad's tumble, I suggested to Jack that we leave early for the city because I wanted to visit him in his nursing home. I also had a two o'clock doctor's appointment, and, somewhere in between, we needed to pick up a few groceries before meeting our friends to drive to Niagara-on-the-Lake for dinner and the play.

"Sounds like a bit much," he said. "Do you really have to do everything in one day? Getting up before dawn won't work for me. Can't you just ease back in?"

"Well, I haven't seen my dad in six days—"

"Yes, I know that, but you're not his only daughter."

"Yeah well, I'd also like to drop in at the house. See how things are going there."

"So, you're saying you want to check in on Jacquelin."

I shifted in my seat. "Yeah. Sorry. I haven't heard from her and that worries me a bit."

I hadn't felt up to reminding him I'd asked both sisters for help getting our dad to his new nursing home. I'd suggested it would work well if one daughter was in the ambulance and the other waiting for him at the nursing home.

"We don't want him arriving to a strange place with no family around him."

Jacquelin had written me a text that said, "I have a doctor's appointment."

I hoped her appointment was with the therapist I helped her find. As far as I knew, she liked the woman, a point I embraced with a thankful heart. Some people would say there were not many women whom my sister liked.

Mel's text had been longer: "No Bev. I am not available to help. You and J live 10 - 20 minutes away...I've attempted to discuss this issue on a number of occasions and frankly I have felt unheard. I'm not able to be part of the everyday help now that Dad is going to be further into the city. I will visit my father in the way I am able...and continue my loving relationship with him..." Fifteen minutes later, she added: "Grow up and order an ambulance, Bev."

Okay then. She couldn't have been any clearer.

Still, four years later I wonder if I made a mistake by not sending Mel the letter I'd drafted in my journal on August 16.

Mel, I am writing this note to you because we have lost the capacity to talk to one another for more than ten minutes without getting into conflict. You probably don't disagree. Of late, we have been communicating about one thing we have in common — we both love our father and we're grieving the loss of his full health. Given this commonality, it seems we'd communicate with ease. I wonder where we went wrong. I can't clearly name what's going on for us but I think it's been stewing for a long time. Sometimes it takes a crisis to bring things to a head. That crisis could be Dad's health and hospitalization. ...

[Journal entry, August 16, 2017].

Twenty-eight
The Ending as the Beginning

September 5 - 6, 2017

Jack and I managed to get down to Toronto with enough time to do almost everything I wanted to do, except see Jacquelin. While he stayed home with the dogs, I saw my doctor and went to the nursing home to see my dad. Jack picked up the groceries. When I got off the nursing home's elevator, the first person I saw was mopping the tile floor. I could smell a strong cleaning solution. She wore a name badge, which told me her name was Faith. As I passed by and said hello, I wondered if the scent of the cottage's wood fire lingered from my clothing and hair. The glare from fluorescent lights did nothing to diminish my harried mood. In the lounge, two women sat side by side near the window. They weren't looking out, nor were they talking to one another. They just stared into the space around them. A frail-looking woman sat at a table with a jigsaw puzzle with extra-large pieces. Three other women and a man watched a game show on the television mounted on the wall. There was another man sound asleep in his chair. In the middle of the room, a nurse prepared meds at her cart.

"Are you looking for someone?" The personal support worker wore a bright orange smock. His badge told me his name—Caesar.

"Yes, I'm looking for my dad…"

"Fred?"

"Yes—"

He pointed, "There he is…there's Fred." Caesar's enthusiasm appealed to me.

My dad was by himself in the far corner facing a large window with a leafy-green view.

When he heard Caesar say his name, he lifted his head and looked in our direction. His face filled with colour and so did his voice.

"Howdy...you're here—"

"Yes Dad, I'm here. It's so good to see you."

"It's very good to meet you, Beverley," said Caesar. "Now I've met all three of your father's daughters—you, Melody and Jacquelin."

My dad looked comfortable in his wheelchair. He was wearing his cozy blue sweatshirt, the one with a picture of a large-breed dog and a caption that read, "My Dog Walks All Over Me."

"Good to see you in my favourite shirt."

Grinning, he brushed his large hand across his chest and looked over at Caesar, "My daughter bought me this shirt."

"Yes," I said, "I picked it up from the gift shop at the Toronto Humane Society."

He smiled again and said he remembered. Caesar agreed it was a very nice shirt.

One of the nurses came over to introduce herself. The closer she got, the wider her smile. The long strands of dark-brown hair fell from a perfect bun and framed her round face.

"Hello, I'm Barbara." We shook hands, and I liked her right away.

She was the nurse who had called the night before when we were still at the cottage.

Barbara told me my dad had taken a fall. A personal support worker found him on the floor. Apparently, he was attempting to get out of bed on his own. The call had come in late. It left me feeling worried and sleepless.

Relieved that my father's complexion had become rosier, I turned to Barbara. "My dad's looking pretty good, don't you think?" The sweatshirt accentuated his blue eyes and made them look bright. His skin was clean and moist, and someone had combed his fine hair.

"Yes, and he's got a strong will," said Barbara. "Your dad's gonna be with us for long time." I loved her warm words. In one of our later conversations, Barbara told me my dad reminded her of her own father and of his strong will to live. I liked her story a lot.

"Dad, so now that we all agree you're good-looking, how are you feeling?"

Barbara laughed and he chuckled. "Oh, not so bad." Looking at Barbara, he added, "Do you think my daughter can have a cup of coffee?"

"Certainly—"

He knew Jack was in his second round of chemo and asked me about how things were going.

"The treatments go pretty well," I said. "He sleeps a lot afterwards and I have to find new ways to get him to eat. He's lost a lot of weight."

"He's always had a good appetite—"

"Yeah, it's unbelievable how that's changed."

I told him we'd just driven in from the cottage and, that after the visit, Jack and I were going with friends to see a play called *Middletown*.

"That's nice," he said. "I haven't seen Jacquelin in a while."

"She didn't come and see you over the weekend?"

"No."

"I'll give her a call, Dad, and see what's up."

On the way out of the building, I called Jacquelin and left another voicemail message.

"Hi Jacq. We're back in Toronto. Just leaving Dad's now…give me a call when you have a chance."

Before starting the engine, I sat for a moment. There was so much about my dad's new residence I didn't like. The narrow corridor to his room was lined with wheelchairs and complicated-looking lifts and other medical equipment. The hallway appeared to be the place where tired and unused stuff went to die. The dated three-storey nursing home, with only one elevator, hadn't been my first choice. In that moment, I recognized my glass-half-empty attitude. I wasn't acknowledging two people I already liked—Caesar and Barbara—and how they engaged with my dad. I also thought of Faith and, later, whenever our paths crossed, she was always with a mop and her kind eyes reached out to me.

Sitting in the car, I thought about the schedule I'd prepared in hopes of coordinating "daughter and granddaughter" visits with our dad.

I asked myself why didn't Jacquelin show up. Did she bail because she was with Howie?

The visits were extra-important because my dad was somewhere he didn't want to be. He seemed discombobulated after the twenty-one-day stay in the hospital, most of which hadn't gone well. After arguing with the social worker, I wrestled with the administration. I wanted my father to have more physiotherapy than the social worker and the two physiotherapists were willing to schedule. When they told me he was too weak, I pointed at the times on his chart when they assessed him. They did their evaluations when my dad was dehydrated.

The doctor kept telling us my father's age, like that was supposed to be the reason to not offer any rehabilitation. The other thing that bothered us was that the social worker was bent on discharging him. By the end of his stay, Mel and I were incensed that our father had gone into the hospital walking, albeit with a walker, and came out in a wheelchair. Therefore, it was under duress and with a solid dose of determination that I went looking for the best nursing home.

One time, I'd talked Jacquelin into accompanying me. "I've got appointments for tours at three nursing homes today and it would really help if you'd come with me."

She did, and, even though she hardly said a word, I could tell the experience was as difficult for her as it was for me. She was not only quieter than usual, she picked at her fingernails, which for Jacquelin, was always a giveaway when she was feeling anxious. We both assumed our father would be living in his own home until the end of his life. Isn't that what everyone wants? The new reality was hard enough, but for Jacquelin there was something more. Now that my dad's time living in his own home was coming to an end, Jacquelin had to be wondering what that meant for her. She had no extra cash, no job, and no house of her own. Did she see herself staying on in our father's house?

"Jacquelin, if and when Dad's house goes on the market, I'll help you find a place to live." I wanted to put her mind at rest. "You'll always have a roof over your head. Whatever happens, Dad's still going to help you out financially."

For her, there was a lot of ambiguity. Unbeknown to her or anyone else, I had my sights on a small, dog-friendly, two-storey-walk-up not far from me. A safe, central neighbourhood, I thought, with my help around the corner.

After we toured all three nursing homes, I invited her to lunch.

"It's on me."

As I drove west on Eglinton, she pointed to a Mary Brown's Fried Chicken.

I responded, "How about somewhere a little nicer? Let's go to Glow, at Shops at Don Mills." I wanted to treat her to something special.

It was a warm day, so we sat on the patio overlooking a courtyard where in the winter there was an ice rink. She ordered a hamburger and helped herself to lots of my salad. It was good to see her eating, but I was struck by how she devoured her food.

Our lunch conversation wasn't easy. She was reserved, careful, and uncertain. A couple of times she left the table to smoke. I cringed when she tossed her butt on the ground. From a distance I could see her tremble.

On top of our father having to move into a nursing home, I could tell how the interviews for the proposal writer job had stressed her out. Jacquelin was convinced that getting this job would change her life.

After the fourth interview, she was asked to submit a proposal in response to the case they sent her. Impressed with her submission, she was told that they wanted to make her an offer. But first, she had to consent to a background check.

At lunch, her hands shook. From her words and how she looked I was sure her thinking was lodged in the notion that things could go wrong. I tried to inhale her apprehension, so she wouldn't have to deal with it all on her own. Our conversation circled around the background check. The company's request had sent Jacquelin into a tailspin. She was worried about her impaired driving charge, which meant she had a criminal record.

"Tell the truth," I said. "You're sober now."

My words didn't help. Eating lunch on a sunny patio didn't help. Being in the midst of lots of wealthy people shopping didn't help. As I drove away, I wondered if I'd made a mistake by not considering Jacquelin's suggestion about going to a fast-food joint.

Before I dropped her back off at Dad's, I had asked her if she felt okay about being in the house on her own. She reminded me that she had Siron. Her words made me chuckle. I still wonder if she noticed that she could make me laugh.

On the busy September 5th day, home from the cottage, and after the visit with Dad, I sat in my car near the nursing home. I didn't need to look at the schedule. Mel was in Halifax for a wedding, and I knew it was Jacquelin's turn to spend time with our dad. In truth, I created the schedule to alleviate my own guilt about abandoning him in an institutional home. I thought if each daughter took a turn, everyone would be doing the right thing by spending time with him. By now, both sisters likely thought me controlling. Perhaps so, but I wanted to know he'd have the company of at least one of his three daughters over the long weekend.

At our lunch on the patio at Glow, I remember saying to Jacquelin, "Maybe it's good you'll be spending some time with dad this weekend. A distraction might help you relax a bit."

My dad was my rock, even when he wasn't at his best. Could she not see he was her rock too? I had convinced myself that Jacquelin staying home over the long weekend to check in on our dad at the nursing home might give her comfort. I also thought her commitment to spend time with him would keep away from Boy Toy, the man no one in our family wanted her to hang with.

I'm not sure how long I sat parked on the street near the nursing home. I had enough time to admire the old trees. Almost every front yard had one. Being under the canopy of leaves helped to ground me. Holding my sister's life in my heart and soul, I asked for a little extra help. *Please God, let this happen. She has worked hard and she really needs this job. It's a lifesaver.*

I took the small notebook from my purse. I wanted to make another list of things my father needed:

- buy track pants for Dad
- ear phones for D's television
- pick up Hudson Bay blanket from the house

I flipped over the page and started another list, "To Do."

- call Jacquelin—not answering phone
- follow-up with nurse about sore on Dad's right arm
- ask about urine sample result—<u>tomorrow</u>
- Dad wants catheter out!!

***

After the visit with my dad and my medical appointment, Jack and I met our friends Jon and Michael and headed to Niagara.

All the way along the Queen Elizabeth Way and into the small streets of Niagara-on-the-Lake, I mulled over my sister's situation and checked my phone.

From Jon's back seat, I said, "She's still not responding to my texts or calls."

Someone suggested her phone could be out of power.

"A distinct possibility," I said, mindful of her chaotic life.

But she wasn't answering the landline either. To comfort myself, I wrapped my arms around my stomach.

"She could be anywhere," said Jack, reaching over to squeeze my hand.

True enough. I thought about the dog park. When she was down there, she turned off her phone, something I thought odd given anything can happen in an off-leash park, especially one isolated behind Sunnybrook Hospital. My sister's logic never ceased to baffle me.

I ran the palm of my hand over the smoothness of the seat.

"This is beautiful leather," I told Jon.

"Yeah, thanks."

Jack chuckled, "Sweetie, you're riding in a top-of-the-line Lexus."

Jon sounded apologetic, "It's a lease."

"Leather's great when you have a dog," I said.

Jon looked at me in the rear-view mirror. "Really?"

"Oh yeah. Easier than fabric. Leather you can just wipe off. My Prelude has leather but not as supple like this. Jacquelin's Audi has leather too."

"Yeah, I know. My last lease was that same model. Good little SUV. That's costing her a couple of bucks."

I knew what he was thinking. Jacquelin was unemployed.

"She paid cash for it," I said. "Bought it with money from the sale of her house."

I remembered the conversation in my dad's living room. He did his best to convince Jacquelin not to buy a European car, one that was expensive to maintain. She told us it was her dream car.

I explained to Jon and Michael that my dad had been paying her mortgage until he decided it wasn't a good idea. "He told her she could live with him rent-free and he'd help her with paying off her debts."

"That was good of him," said Jon.

"Yeah, at the time I thought it was a win-win. My dad was living alone in his large bungalow. The idea was that she could save money, look for a job, and get back on her feet. But it was more than that. He wanted to help turn her life around."

I didn't say how else she spent her money. Lots of cosmetic surgery. Some people thought she looked like the actress Julia Roberts.

I had asked her once why she thought she needed rhinoplasty. "You have a perfect nose."

"It's too pointy." Apparently her grade three teacher had said so.

Closing my eyes and leaning against the back seat, I pictured the time I invited her to the evening service at Saint James Cathedral on Queen Street. I was hoping the tranquil space would bring her a little comfort, peace, and serenity. That's how it worked for me. I explained to Jacquelin how the physical structure of worn pews eased the ache in my upper back. I relished the relief, if only for a short time. I told her that when I was sitting in a church alone, I liked to hear the safe whispers in the background. I would feel connected to something outside myself.

While we sat in the cathedral a tall slender woman wearing black leather pants stumbled to our pew and asked for money.

I tucked a little cash into her gloved hand, and she went away.

"She's having a hard time," Jacquelin said. I heard pain in her whisper.

"Yes."

Her empathy, I thought, was a good sign. Unlike in the past, I didn't hear any judgement. I wondered if Jacquelin saw herself in the woman. The thought made my stomach rumble.

Sitting in the comfort of Jon's back seat, I thought about Jacquelin's preoccupation with the background check required by the interviewing company.

"Do you think an impaired driving charge will show up on a background check?"

"Probably," said Jon.

"It would. It's a criminal offence," said Michael. He sounded sure.

"Yeah, but do you think it would matter to an employer who's looking for a proposal writer?"

"Depends on the company. Where has she applied?"

"It's a large life insurance company," I said. "Financial and health insurance. They're in the business of health, including mental health."

"Probably then. I think those companies are pretty rigid," said Jon, catching my eye in his rear-view mirror.

"It's not like she robbed a bank," said Michael.

"No. True. It's not like that," I whispered.

The four of us talked about how we humans can also be decent and give others second chances.

Please God, let us be right...

I sent Jacquelin another text to remind her not to give up on people and not to give up on herself.

From the car window I looked out onto Lake Ontario. The water looked choppy. In the momentum of the moving car, scenes from my sister's life ran through my brain.

Jon said, "You're really worried about her."

"Yeah, I am." I sent her another text. "Jacquelin, other people get through things like this. You will too."

She needed to get back into the workforce but I wasn't convinced she was ready for the complexities of the job she was going after.

At the same time, her present job of working in a doggie daycare wasn't good for her either. Jacquelin, a forever advocate for the fair and humane treatment of animals, advised me against ever taking my dogs to that particular organization. She didn't agree with their policies (I didn't get the details) and didn't respect the woman who owned the business.

"They give the worst jobs and hours to me even though I've been there longer than some other people."

That was hard for me to hear. "Why do you think your boss is doing that?"

"She'd rather give the students the hours."

Inferring she was undervalued, I pictured how my sister presented herself—fragile and unhappy— and I had a hunch that could have shaped her employer's response. The more I heard, the more things didn't sound right. I spoke to my dad about my concerns.

"Dad, I think this job is killing her."

He agreed, and we both thought she should quit. She did, but not right away. My sister had a work ethic.

After the play and a follow-up chat in the foyer with the actors, we drove back to Toronto. If the men discussed the play, I was too full of angst to listen. I checked my phone a lot and each time deepened the bad feeling in my stomach.

Back in the Leslieville parking lot where the four of us had met almost seven hours earlier, Jack and I said goodbye to Michael and thanked Jon again for the evening.

"It was a real treat, Jon. Thank you so much," I said.

I would have enjoyed it more had my sister answered my calls or texted me back.

***

Once buckled into Jack's jeep, we pulled out of the lot.

"I want to go over to my dad's house. Check in on Jacquelin. You okay with that?"

"Sure. We can do that."

It was 12:30 in the morning.

Seeking a diversion, I said, "I thought *Middleton* was an excellent performance. Great writing."

I could tell Jack had liked it because for most of the performance he was on the edge of his seat. He also enjoyed meeting the cast afterward in the foyer. I asked about the conversation he'd had with the lead actor.

"We talked about the role."

"Powerful—"

"Yeah, and tough. He said, 'After every show I go home and die.'"

"Remember what the cop said to the audience at the end? It tore my heart out. *You think you know people. You don't. You think you caught some non-suicidal gleam in their eye. You didn't. You never know what people are going to do.*"

Relieved to be back in the city on our way home and closer to freeing my brain from worry, I said, "Yeah, that character...he didn't have much of a will to live...that was a long death...did you see that coming?"

Leaving that question unanswered, we turned into Dad's driveway, to the sight of Jaquelin's treasured black Audi, gleaming in the moonlight, and to make our final, tragic discovery for the night...

To the Moon
Art thou pale for weariness
Of climbing heaven and gazing on the earth
Wandering companionless
Among the starts that have a different birth,
And every changing, like a joyless eye
That finds no object worth its constancy?

Percy Bysshe Shelley
1792 - 1822

Epilogue
Lessons in the Light

There has been nothing darker in my life than Jack's fourth stage cancer and his doctor's end-of-life diagnosis, and finding my youngest sister dead after her suicide. Though their vulnerabilities were different, their journeys overlapped. How I walked with each of them was not the same. Jack wanted to live. Jacquelin didn't.

It did not take until the end of Jacquelin's life for me to realize I'd been losing myself in her story. Her struggles filled my head. I thought every song, poem or newscast I heard was about her. I saw Jacquelin on street corners when it wasn't her. She was everywhere. As her despair waned back and forth and loitered at the edges of seedy darkness, I hovered on the sideline. I remember how hard it was to try and steer her away from people I was sure would do her no good. How did I judge which people were bad for her? Was I projecting my own life experiences onto my youngest sister? For the longest time I didn't think so, but the deeper my excavation into our relationship, the more I saw my earlier unexamined self.

A few weeks after my sister's death, I told my dad that I planned to write a memoir about my journey with Jacquelin.

He looked into my eyes. "Do it." His fingers touched his chin. "Yeah, do it."

My father's words felt like a blessing and I set out on a path of rediscovering self.

Writing this memoir brought up hard questions. Did Jacquelin push me away because she sensed I knew how close she was to the edge? My compulsion to save her was fueled by love. What else? Was

I doing what my mother had taught me to do so many years earlier? That is, step in and assist with mothering? And by being there for my sister, was there some element of saving my mom as well?

Had I been Jacquelin's birth mother and not just her older sister by eleven years, I might have had an easier time describing the depth of love I felt for her. In a Sunday morning homily, Reverend Canon Janet Read-Hockin used the word "splagchnizomai," and after the service, I looked it up. Splagchnizomai means "to be moved so deeply by something that you feel it in the pit of your stomach." I mentioned the word earlier and again here because it captures the intensity of my emotional attachment to my youngest sister. Reverend Janet's homily was timely because I had been grappling with memories of Jacquelin's sharp barbs and how they pushed me away. The word splagchnizomai seized the essence of how I continued to feel about my sister despite her deplorable behaviour. I did not stop trying to find ways to get through her armoured wall. I wanted to be in her life whether she wanted me there or not. I took responsibility for making that happen. I thought I was good for her.

Mostly I bounced against her hardness and pretended to be strong. Inside, I was melting. I could not walk away, especially when she was in trouble. From the get-go, I was pulled to watch over her and that's something that did not change during our shared lifetimes. Since her beginning, it was love at first sight. Full stop.

I examined how Jacquelin and I moved in and out of friendship and other relationships livable between sisters. Probing into our relationship over a breadth of time stirred me up. Among those stirrings, was loneliness. Before she died, I'd been missing her and I fought hard to salvage our relationship. Alcoholism, and maybe an undiagnosed mental health illness, played havoc with a lifegiving relationship.

A friend asked if I had the chance to help again would I do anything different? I liked her question because it gave me pause to ask, "What did I learn?" She was asking on behalf of a distraught friend who was concerned about her adult son's drug addiction. I reflected on her question. Do I recommend sitting in the dark watching a loved one's house from the street? Would I again be quick to drive to a seedy motel to coax a loved one into the safety of my car? Would I go alone? When a man screams at me to come and collect my "loser" sister because he has used her up, would I run to her rescue?

My response to questions involving rescue would be "yes" but with a caveat. I wouldn't go alone. But I'd need someone to help, someone who wouldn't judge my sister or her situation, someone to be patient enough to wait out Jacquelin's reluctance to respond. I could have asked my friend Joyce, but that would have meant waking up her household at some ungodly hour, which felt like too much. Had Jack been well, I would have urged him to come with me to the motel, the west-end coffee shop, and other places. But I know he would not have tolerated waiting outside Jacquelin's house.

I would mention to the burdened mother that getting lost inside a loved one's brokenness can be wearisome. I was fatigued, fragile, and full of uncertainty and self-criticism. I fought disillusionment. I used my journal as a confidant. I talked a lot to Jack.

When it came my way, I did embrace support from the community. I'm so glad I followed through on the advice of the woman from Victim Services. Had I not, I would not have encountered the pivotal experience at the Suicide Loss Survivor program with Alex, Edgar and Liz. I was fortunate to work in CBT, cognitive behavioural therapy, with two different therapists—Dr. Denisoff, soon after the shock of Jacquelin's death, and Dr. Maddocks, at the onset of writing my memoir. I hope anyone grieving suicide loss finds someone to talk to like I did. This person might be a therapist or a trusted friend. When it came to the notion of healing and not going it alone, I made my choices knowing that I needed to be in a relationship—professional or social— that resembled a genuine friendship, with qualities of trust and listening.

In the turmoil and uncertainty of Jack's cancer that coincided with Jacquelin's turbulence, he and I found ways to take time for ourselves. We went to the cottage between treatments and oncology appointments. The travel time between the two places was good for letting go and those uninterrupted chats were important. In the wintertime, a crackling fire in the woodstove set the stage to preserve simplicity between rifts of chaos. At the cottage, I breathed more deeply. Slept better too. I had an easier time letting go. Those "time-outs" helped to replenish my weary soul. Jack's too. We were also grateful to have our sanctuary by the lake among the pines.

In the city, I had a routine. It worked for me to exercise three or four times a week in the all-purpose room at my church. Small talk in the foyer and moving to music in instructed classes was a significant tendril to my lifeline. I never forgot my doctor's wise words, "Those exercise classes are as important to you as Jack's oncology appointments are to him."

I was in a book club and I tried not to miss monthly meetings where we treated each other with special foods and good wine. Cancer, alcoholism, or long-term care were never central topics at book club. Our conversations weren't light, but for me book club time was a no-problem zone.

It mattered to surround myself with authentic people whether for a walk through the woods or lunch on a patio. I liked it a lot when I crossed paths with my favourite dog walker friend in the ravines with her cohort. Chaos sometimes ensued among some of the dogs, but mostly it was a short-lived misunderstanding and easily resolved. Oftentimes, the rascals among the pack made me laugh.

I dabbled in writing fiction. One short story evolved into a suspense novel. Writing it distracted me from the realities of my own life. I developed characters from the ground up and I made their lives as flawed and complicated as I wanted. I met with my critique group every second week. Discussions rarely touched on our non-writing lives. Some writers in my larger writing community knew Jack was unwell. I was less vocal about Jacquelin. When she died, heart-felt cards fell through the mail slot, and my in-box filled with beautifully worded notes. I placed the cards everywhere in the house and cherished every word of support.

There are few perfect paths in recovery from addiction. To cope, I listened to my heart and followed with my feet. I caution anyone not to expect perfection. Loving someone who is in trouble is a messy learning curve.

Through personal excavation into my younger years, I gained insight into the patterns of "tiptoeing" prevalent in my family. My mother, who was also a fearful person, used to imply Jacquelin was never wrong. For example, if Jacquelin had been reprimanded at work, my mother declared the problem stemmed from jealousy over her daughter's good looks.

I'd go out on a limb and say, "Mom, even if that is true, there's likely more to it."

My mother looked away, which meant the conversation was over.

In my work life, I counselled students not to reside in denial or secrets. I believe my career choice might have been a way of breaking from family patterns. When I risked asking questions beyond the family code, I was outside the unspoken-family rule. I came to understand part of how that code evolved. My father knew of my mother's fears. When she didn't want to learn how to drive a car, he let that be. When she didn't want to stay at the cottage with us girls but without him, he was okay with that too. Rightly or wrongly, he protected her, and she felt safe with him. No wonder my mother wanted nothing more for each of her three daughters than to "have a man." My dad and I talked about some of this after she was gone. We also spoke about how much Jacquelin was like my mother.

After my mother left us, there was no code of silence in my chats with Dad. We spoke freely. Identifying and breaking from my family's pattern brought me relief, and I feel freed up to be honest and genuine with others. I am no longer burdened by family secrets.

In hindsight, I believe my mother recognized Jacquelin's fragility. She was protecting her daughter. Both of us wanted Jacquelin to thrive, but how we went about it clashed. Why did Mom feel compelled to keep her fear about Jacquelin's fragility secret? Did my mother not know me well enough to tell me? Was distrust embedded in her unspoken fear? Lots of questions. At my dad's bedside, when I shared thoughts about my mother's fears, he nodded. Did a mother's unspoken fears feed the family code of silence? The code was not just about Jacquelin's fragility. We were maintaining my mother's serenity too. More protection.

***

Like the disease of cancer, mental unwellness is sneaky and scary. On the screen of an MRI machine, the tumours in Jack's brain moved around a lot and some of the thirteen tumours weren't always visible to the trained eye. Tumours hid. I recall when one of Jack's oncologists said, "I can't see it, but I know it's there." Fortunately, the oncologist found the sneaky cancer cell that tried to hide. It was in the centre of Jack's left lung.

Mental unwellness can also hide. In Jacquelin's youth, was she experiencing developmental mood swings or could it have been her serotonin was low? When I read about bipolar symptoms, I recognized Jacquelin's struggles. To the best of my knowledge, Jacquelin was never diagnosed, but if she was, she didn't tell us about it, and it is not my place to say with any certainty that Jacquelin was bipolar. Was she content? When Jacquelin suffered from migraines, there was little ambivalence about being physically sick. When it came to her mental illness, the same clarity did not apply.

My dad left us twenty-nine months after Jacquelin died. His death was peaceful. Seven years earlier at her bedside in the ICU, he had told my mother that he would see her "on the other side." I'm grateful he waited long enough, so he and I could be at each other's sides for a while longer.

Reverend Ian officiated at the funeral. The church filled with cousins and friends. I felt blessed to have helped shape a wonderful funeral to celebrate his full life. It was held one day before the Anglican diocese closed their churches due to the Covid-19 pandemic. Later in the spring, when it was safe to gather outside, Reverend Janet officiated at the internment of my father's ashes into the grave of my mother. As I had done for my mother, I tucked a picture of my sisters and me into his grave.

Reverend Janet was kind to bring daffodil bulbs for Mel, Marianne and me. Up north, I planted the bulbs in crevices of the rock garden behind my writing cabin so I could see their blooms from the window.

At the internment at the cemetery I talked about Zachary, one of our black labs. Within seconds, Zachary got down on his belly and rolled on the fresh soil covering the side-by-side graves of my mother and sister. I'd never heard him moan and cry like that before, and his unapologetic grief tugged at my heart. The next day, I returned to the graves with my friend Diane. The sun was disappearing through the trees and a large deer with full antlers, was grazing on ground-cover. When she looked up her eyes fixed on me and she sauntered in our direction.

I whispered to Diane, "What do think she wants?"

Diane shuddered and said, "I have no idea."

The deer was unafraid. She was closest to me, and I felt anxious. I sensed she was holding a message. She was large and strong and determined to reach me. I got spooked and wish now I hadn't felt afraid.

"I think we should go," I said.

"Yeah. I think you're right."

How I wished I had stayed. How I'd love to see her again. How I'd love to see Jacquelin again. In a way, writing this memoir has allowed me to live a second life with my sister.

Three months after my father's death, Jack and I talked seriously about moving out of the city. Jack's immunotherapy had gone so well that one oncologist nicknamed him her "poster-patient" and in a more recent follow-up (September, 2022) she referred to him as "an anomaly." With Jack's improved health, the time felt right. We sold our Toronto house and moved to Muskoka with our dogs. I rejoined a choir and, after feeling that I had lost my voice, I'm singing again.

Making the cottage my fulltime home had been my life dream, and now I am living it. Where I live, the sky feels bigger. On a clear dark night, I see stars, including the moon. In the night's air I stand with her, my friend who was with me in the early hours after my sister's death. The story isn't over, and in the light of the moon, my path is illuminated. The full moon continues to shed her warm light onto a path that helps me find my way. Her gift nurtured a writing journey that brought me back home to myself.

I have no idea if Jacquelin was mindful of the moon's fullness on the night she ended her life. I do know how the moonlight enveloped me from dark to light. I felt held. I witnessed darkness being lifted by light. Now when I look up to see the moon, I think to myself, "Oh there you are, friend. Thank you so much for coming."

Acknowledgements

Dr. Eilenna Denisoff, who said my story needs to be told for families.

Dr. Sarah Maddocks, whose narrative insights made me feel at home in this excavation.

My Awesome Critique Group—Nancy Beal, David Patterson and Simon Hally, for our bi-weekly meetings that preceded writing this memoir. Simon, for extra editorial attention on two early chapters.

Brian Henry, for listening to me read that extra chapter.

Sophia Apostol at Firefly for curiosity behind emotion, leading to fresh insights.

Rick Book, for reading, followed by intense conversations that I love so much.

Gail Lindsay, for regular presence, deep reading, narrative inquisitiveness into the hard questions that unveiled more and for critiques that moved me forward.

Shane Joseph, my publisher who believed enough in the work to take on this project. Your comments deepened my excavation.

Friends and acquaintances whose names are not included but know your presence shaped my lived experience. Individuals whose names are on these pages.

My sister Melody walked the hard journey too, and of course Jacquelin left the story behind for me to tell.

My Dad.

Jack, partner in life, for giving me the space to write while still being there all of the time and whenever I needed you.

Bibliography

Alcoholics Anonymous - Big Book (1993). Alcoholics Anonymous World Services.

Carr, M. (1995). *The Liar's Club*. Viking Adult.

Durkheim, E. *Suicide* (1897/1952). Routledge and Kegan.

Eno, P. W. *Middletown* (2010). Theatre Communications Group, Inc.

Gillmor, G. (2019). *To the River: Losing My Brother*. Penguin Random House, Canada.

Mehler Paperny, A. (2020). *Hello I want to Die Please Help Me*. The Experiment.

Redfield-Jamison, K. (1995). *The Unquiet Mind*. Alfred A. Knopf, Inc.

Shields, C. (2002). *Unless*. Random House, Canada.

Toews, T. (2014). *All My Puny Sorrows*. Alfred A. Knopf, Inc.

Light, Gordon. (1985). "She Comes Sailing on the wind" in the Common Praise Hymnal.

Gillard, Richard. (1987). "The Servant Song" in the Common Praise Hymnal.

<u>Website Resources:</u>

Al-Anon https://al-alon.org

Al-Anon Alateen.on.ca

Canadian Mental Health Association (CAMH) website ontario.cmha.ca

Behavioural Cognitive Therapy Institute.

Crisis Lines—Canada; USA.

Distress Center of Greater Toronto: 416-408-4357; https://dcog.com

Author Bio

Beverley was born and raised in Ontario, Canada. Toronto was her home until she moved to her Muskoka cottage in 2021 with her husband Jack and their two black labs.

Bev graduated from the University of Toronto with the notion of becoming a teacher, a missionary or a social worker. Her introduction to life skills teaching methodology and group facilitation set the stage for her life's work. At Seneca College, Bev's life skills groups supported adult students in job readiness and academic upgrading. When Bev took a position in the social service worker diploma program at Seneca, she taught what she loved doing—group work and counselling. She enrolled in a Bachelor of Education in Adult Education at Brock University and later had the privilege of teaching in the program. With an appetite whet for deep learning, she entered into the department of Curriculum and Teacher

Development at the Ontario Institute for Studies in Education at the University of Toronto and acquired a Master of Education. An introduction to narrative inquiry and personal experience research methods incited her in-depth study into how **friendship shapes learning at the college level.** In her doctoral thesis, Bev defended the significance of navigating relationship and community in the learning experience. After she attained her PhD Bev joined the Teacher Development team at Seneca. Bev retired in her thirty-sixth year of teaching and learning in the community college system. In retirement, Bev writes short-fiction, and completed her first psychological character-driven novel, **No One Knew**. Her second large project is **Dance into the Light**, a memoir. When she's not writing, you can find her in a kayak and when the water freezes over, on snowshoes somewhere on the lake. She's happy to have found like-minded friends who like to sing, hike and play pickle ball year-round.

Printed in the USA
CPSIA information can be obtained
at www.ICGtesting.com
JSHW011407260823
47205JS00004B/7